for a man to carry. Like other good men, he has that strong internal compass to guide that pull back to being the man he knows he can be."
—Rich Tosi, co-founder of The ManKind Project; co-founder of A Couples Weekend

"*At Death Do Us Part* is a beautiful testament and memorial to an extraordinary woman through deep realizations of love and relationship. The experience of reading *At Death Do Us Part* reminds me of a Buddhist, bare-bones, practice of just showing up for what is, with no place to hide. This is not an easy read; yet, it is an important undertaking that evokes within the reader the courage that was necessary to share this narrative."
—Dr. Timothy P Dukes, author of *The Present*

Praise for *At Death Do Us Part*

"Most people know Frederick Marx from *Hoop Dreams*, *Journey From Zanskar*, and other fine films. They probably don't know that he is a longtime student of dharma, an ordained Zen priest, and a gifted writer exploring the terrain of the human heart. This book shivers with the frailties of what it means to be human, enfolding loss in all its forms, finding a way through acceptance and the pure ground of being back to love."

—Ram Dass, author of *Be Here Now*

"This book is one's man's story of love, loss, and realization; actually it is a story that many of us know or will know. Heartbreaking, beautiful, intimate, challenging… this is a book we should all read."

—Rev. Joan Jiko Halifax, author of *Shaman: The Wounded Healer*

"Frederick Marx has written a touchingly intimate account of love, loss and healing. Losing a loved one is something most everyone faces at some point in life. *At Death Do Us Part* shows the possibility of navigating through this journey with consciousness, understanding, and an open heart."

—James Baraz, co-founding teacher Spirit Rock Meditation Center, Woodacre, California; co-author of *Awakening Joy: 10 Steps to Happiness.*

"Raw and beautiful, this tender, joyous look into the shared intimacy of a mature couple, seems almost too secret to put into words. I felt touched so many times in so many ways by this unique wisdom-teaching. As I slowly read the book, I kept falling in love with Frederick. His utterly fearless transparency constantly endeared him to me."

—Bill Kauth, co-founder of The ManKind Project; co-author of *A Circle of Men* and *We Need Each Other*

"*At Death Do Us Part* is a book about life, of change, of opening your heart. Reading Frederick's words and mulling over his stories, I feel that my world is now filled with more depth and more flavors, as well as some new questions and insights about this thing we call being alive. A beautiful, moving book."

—Marc Lesser, author of *Less: Accomplishing More By Doing Less*

"I was deeply moved by Frederick's story beginning with the words from his introduction. 'How do you get over losing your life partner?' This is an experience none of us want to go through, yet it is one that is part of the inevitable human journey. Frederick offers us a glimpse into our present and future losses, but does it in such a beautiful and caring way, we feel like we're with a true guide and loving friend who is holding us in his kind embrace."

—Jed Diamond, author of
My Distant Dad: Healing the Family Father Wound

"How to express how deeply I am touched by this remarkable tale of the truth of living and dying? This is not just an autobiography and history of [their] time together and its cancerous ending, but also a Buddhist dharma teaching. Life and death lived within the Buddhist perspective. It is gift from them to and for all of us. We all need to come to compassionate understanding and radical acceptance of the truth of dying. This book is a great sharing teaching of this understanding."

—JunPo Denis Kelly, Abbot of the Hollow Bones Order of Rinzai Zen

"I have always been aware of Frederick's brilliance, so easy to see in his important documentaries. Now he takes that brilliance once again through the portals of his heart, to share a very intimate, soul-searching book of loss and grief…and beauty and love. All of which can be found in his cracked open heart upon the death of his wife."

—Meredith Little, author & founder of School of Lost Borders

"It's surprisingly enjoyable, moving, captivating, engrossing. Marx revives-reanimates-re-loves–his partner–not as saint, but as person–with textured, reverent, and humorous delight, showing that grief is not a one-way trip to a lugubrious terminus but a single stop on a vast, circuitous journey, a dizzying, dazzling topography filled with aliveness, presence, love."

—Jiwon Chung

"Just like Frederick I've been lost. Like him, Buddhist meditation changed my fundamental perspective on how to approach life, how to deal with failure. There's a level beyond understanding on offer here… Frederick knows that there's a time when being out of integrity, out of wholeness, our internal sense of good, becomes too great a pain

Praise for *Rites to a Good Life*

"The text is filled like a banquet with rituals, stories, medicines, quotes and models, recipes for genuine growth and transformation. This deep connection to the sacred, and to your own unique gifts and courageous place in the world, is what *Rites to a Good Life* and rites of passage remind you is possible. *Rites to a Good Life* is a call for us all to reflect on our own personal journey and its place in the culture and cosmos around us. It is not just for our youth. We need the gifts of these rites at every stage of life and we need ways to continually renew our connection to our deepest purpose and the sacredness of life. I hope this book inspires you to do so."
—Jack Kornfield, author and co-founder of Spirit Rock Meditation Center

"The soothing balm we need in a world on fire. This is the handbook we all need to revive the hero within us with practical and accessible daily rituals for personal growth that just may transform your life and enable you to change those of others."
—Maryann Howland, author of *Warrior Rising*

"Our world is always made easier by rites of passage, and it's made better by this book on the subject. This is a very fine book; thoughtful, well researched and well written."
—Curtis Mitchell

"A fine and important book. The framework provided, the quotes from a range of people and cultures, and the personal story woven in will keep people well involved."
—Meredith Little, author of *The Four Shields: The Initiatory Seasons of Human Nature*

"In *Rites to a Good Life*, Frederick Marx ministers to his readers by slowing them down enough to consider how to craft a life worth living in a hectic and traumatizing world. In so doing, he provides readers the tools to help bring transformation out of trauma, personal depth out of despair, and a life of intentionality out of superficiality. Books like this can recreate readers' worlds."
—Joel Edward Goza, author of *America's Unholy Ghosts: The Racist Roots of our Faith and Politics*

"A powerful and visionary endeavor. Inspiring."
—Joan Halifax, author and founder Upaya Zen Center

"In my years of doing rites of passage work with boys and young men, I've never met anyone with more experience, insight, or passion about those issues than Frederick Marx. All of those qualities come through on virtually every page of this book. Frederick never fails to show respect toward those whose approach to rites of passage may vary from his own. In our culture that has lost the significance of mentoring for both girls and boys, it's the destructive impact we see every day from broken, wounded males that demands crucial attention. Frederick's life work, and this book, have the capacity to bring healing to those wounds."
—Craig Glass, author of *Passage to Manhood: Field Guide*

Praise for *Turds of Wisdom*

"Considering the world as it is, we all need to come to our senses. Our senses of humor! If you don't have a sense of humor (as Wavy Gravy says) it's just not funny. You've got to be kidding!"
—Wes "Scoop" Nisker, author of *Crazy Wisdom*

"What if you could have dinner with a bunch of interesting, wise friends? Let's say you are extremely lucky and you get to invite over an award-winning filmmaker, a deep Buddhist thinker, a funny, somewhat profane trickster and a philosopher with a taste for the absurd. During the dinner they regale you with stories from their lives that are funny, poignant, and useful in equal measure. It would be the meal of a lifetime. This is the book equivalent of that dinner. In the words of Thich Nhat Hanh, 'No Mud, no Lotus.' In the words of Frederick Marx, 'No Turd, no Wisdom.'"
—Bill Duane, former Google Superintendent of Well-Being

"Frederick Marx in his writing, as in his films, shows us the unexpected and delightful path of vulnerability, humor, and wisdom. Great learning more about him, his stories, and his heart."
—Marc Lesser, author of *Seven Practices of a Mindful Leader*

"A riveting journal of experience, truth, and personal wisdom that I digested like baby formula. I found myself reading almost in a child-like state, rapt with the stories. This has got to be helpful, if not entertaining, to a lot of humans, especially men. A great summary of Zen practice and Buddhism in general. Very funny."
—Mike Zanoli, Part-time Cook and Philosopher

"A fun read. A candid, heartfelt, naked presentation of life faced. An inspiring example for me of what being fearless and courageous with my own life's pains and confusions and ignorance can do. May keep the psychiatrist away!"
—Roger Nielson, Auburn Bus Driver

Praise for *Confessions of a Sacred Fool*

"Frederick Marx is a man of whom many will say, 'He's so full of it!' And they'll actually mean wisdom! Let him lead you on a journey. You'll laugh and gasp, and perhaps emerge with a sensibility that is at once deeper and higher."

—Tom Morris, author of *The Oasis Within*

"Marx pulls back the curtain on the Hero's Journey in this humorous and engaging collection of adventures that mixes coming-of-age stories with a life-long spiritual quest. With ironic wit, he recalls rebellious years following deep personal loss and his growing sense of the purpose of art. This book takes on friendship and betrayal, the frailty of belief, and the temptations of fame."

—Tony Evans, author of *Believing in Indians*.

"Marx has once again given himself permission to be raw and go deep while taking on some of life's more difficult issues with all the fumbling grace and self-effacing humility of a Sacred Fool. How did these gems not find their way into the first book? You will be enlightened and entertained."

—Ian Stout, writer and filmmaker

"Frederick Marx's new book is a work of considerable thought and careful self-analysis from which many will gain considerable knowledge. Reminded me of Jonathan Swift's classic *A Modest Proposal*. Without an iota of hubris, Marx is able to synthesize a lifetime of experiences into a confessional that emphasizes the spiritual and practical roads he's traveled. A continuation of a remarkable life story and a must-read."

—Dwayne Johnson-Cochran, writer and filmmaker

"Marx has arrived at a self-expression style that is unique, genre-bending, and refreshing. His premise is similar to that which some meditation/spiritual books put forth: not meant as a serial set of building lessons but a scattershot of insights and experience. To use what is useful and let the rest go."

—Peter Boland, author of *Making Managed Healthcare Work*

CONFESSIONS OF A SACRED FOOL

Absurdities and Wisdom
from a Buddhist Rebel

FREDERICK MARX

This book is sold subject to the condition that it shall not, by way of trade or otherwise, be lent, re-sold, hired out or otherwise circulated without the publisher's prior consent in any form of binding or cover other than that in which it is published and without a similar condition including this condition being imposed on the subsequent purchaser.

Copyright © Frederick Marx 2025

Frederick Marx asserts the moral right to be identified as the author of this work in accordance with the Copyright, Designs and Patents Act, 1988.

Love After Love from
Collected Poems 1948-1984 by Derek Walcott.
Reprinted by permission of Farrar, Straus and Giroux. USA
The Poetry of Derek Walcott 1948-2013 by Derek Walcott.
Reprinted by permission of Faber & Faber, UK
Copyright © 1986 by Derek Walcott.
All Rights Reserved.

ISBN 979-8-9991348-0-6

All rights reserved. No part of this publication may be reproduced, stored in a retrieval system, or transmitted, in any form or by any means, electronic, mechanical, photocopying, recording, or otherwise, without the prior permission of the publisher.

Auburn, CA. 95603

For my mother and father; don't blame them.

Intimacy is the art and practice of living from the inside out.
    —David Whyte

The neurotic is always the most self-informative.
    —Marjorie Rawlings

LOVE AFTER LOVE

The time will come
when, with elation
you will greet yourself
arriving
at your own door, in your
own mirror
and each will smile at the
other's welcome

and say, sit here. Eat.
You will love again the
stranger who was your self.
Give wine. Give bread.
Give back your heart
to itself, to the stranger who
has loved you

all your life, whom you
ignored
for another, who knows you
by heart.
Take down the love letters
from the bookshelf,

the photographs, the
desperate notes,
peel your own image from
the mirror.
Sit. Feast on your life.

—Derek Walcott

Table of Contents

Foreword	1
Preface	3
Introduction	9
Chapter 1: Heyokha!	13
Chapter 2: Being Evil	21
Chapter 3: At Sea	29
Chapter 4: Trying to Pee While a Nurse is Watching	41
Chapter 5: The Boy in the Mirror	45
Chapter 6: More Thoughts on Meaningless Thoughts	51
Chapter 7: Grin-Fucking	57
Chapter 8: Proselytizers	63
Chapter 9: Understanding Projection	69
Chapter 10: Forever Falling	71
Chapter 11: Ghosts Among Us	77
Chapter 12: Sex Gurus Around the World	83
Chapter 13: Living for Posterity	87
Chapter 14: Get Out of the Pool!	91
Chapter 15: Lost in Translation: More China Follies	95
Chapter 16: Why I Will Never Be Politically Correct	107
Chapter 17: I Love My Friends. I Think.	113
Chapter 18: My Life as a Lab Rat	121
Chapter 19: Against Hope	133
Epilogue	139
Thank You for Reading My Book	141
Acknowledgments	143
Other Works by Frederick Marx	145

Foreword

SOMETIMES YOU ARE just not in the mood for Jonathan Franzen. Like this morning. There it sat on my bedside table, *The Corrections*. It's a thick book. It reminded me of those cheeseburgers at high-end restaurants that are taller than they are wide. *Looks great,* I always think, *but how am I going to fit that thing into my mouth?* Such was my mood as I stared at Franzen's tome, which could be measured either in pages or pounds. *How am I going to fit that thing into my brain?*

Luckily I had Frederick Marx's *Confessions of a Sacred Fool: Absurdities and Wisdom from a Buddhist Rebel* downloaded on my iPhone. I opened the file, went into airplane mode, and started reading. I finished the book a few hours later feeling both lighter and more satisfied, as though emerging from my favorite cafe after coffee and conversation with a wonderful friend.

Confessions of a Sacred Fool is a pithy book with tight, clean chapters. Which is to say, it is a gift. Readable, wise, and funny, it roams freely between personal anecdotes and big ideas, taking us through the broad sweep of Marx's life without ever getting bogged down in minutia or argument. In presenting himself so clearly, so simply, Marx gives us room to compliment his reflections with our own. As he remembers, contemplates, and thinks out loud, so do we, for the pleasures of personal writing like this are contagious!

As a writer, Marx is light on his feet, and in real life, he's gotten around. He traveled with the first rock band to ever tour China (no, it wasn't Wham!). He's been to the Oscars and Emmys (an honor to be nominated, not much fun to attend). He tried to film sex gurus around the world (and lived to tell stories about it, of course). Meanwhile, when stationary he prides himself on cultivating relationships with Deep Creatives, like the movie director Harold Ramis, but finds that some of his most interesting companions are the least celebrated. Marx is known for his work in film, notably *Hoop Dreams*, and there are plenty of insights here into cinema, Hollywood, and culture-making in general. But this book is also a useful study of the committed artist who is still, at age sixty-nine, finding his way. Not quite satisfied with his career, with his output, Marx deconstructs his own ambitions, guiding us to an understanding of what truly matters in life, as he himself discovers it right there before us on the page.

Because in the end, this is a book about wisdom. Or Dharma, if you will. Marx is a committed Buddhist practitioner. *Confessions of a Sacred Fool* is shot through with Marx's particular brand of Hollow Bones Zen. He does not lead with sutras, koans, or platitudes, but with his own experience. *Here is what I have done, here is where I have been, here is how I have lived and what I have learned.* Alas, this is the best kind of dharma. The lived-in kind, the kind with fingerprints. Fortunately, it also makes for pleasurable reading! If I want heavy, I'll pick up Franzen. But sometimes, like this morning, I need the generous offerings of a book that's short and sweet. Those mornings are reserved for Marx and his confessions, both sacred and amusing.

—Jack Haubner, March 30, 2025

Preface

THOUGH NOT IN NAME, this is a sequel to my last book *Turds of Wisdom: Real Life Stories from a Buddhist Rebel*. Yes, I had to do Number Two. Inexplicably, I've hit a groove resurrecting celebrated ghosts of my youth, the Art Buchwalds, Mike Roykos, and Russell Bakers, the syndicated newspaper columnists who entranced and amused me. But calling forth these luminaries only goes so far. They would have had the good sense to never title a book, no matter how thematically apropos or tonally jocular, with the word Turds. Continuing down this path I soon would've ended up with Volume 3: *Turds of Wisdom: Explosive Diarrhea*. Funny to me and a few men over 50, but not a ticket to the mainstream. As the saying goes, "You can go your own way," and I've done it for most of my life, but you should never expect success to follow. Fortunately, the voices of non-scatological wisdom got to me, and I went on a hunt for a new title, one that also wouldn't imply that there was anything narratively sequential about the two volumes since they're really just stylistically similar idea collages.

That hunt led some interesting places. First I went back to the reject pile from *Turds*.

- We Become What We Think. Stop Thinking That Shit!
- Impermanence… Where Was I?
- They Say That Waking Up Is Hard to Do…

- Attachment Leads to Suffering. Get Away from Me!
- Ennervana
- Letting Go, Letting God, Letting Goddamn!
- Karma, Shawarma
- Awakening Under the Booty Tree

They're all pretty funny but none of them capture what the book is about. So my partner Maggie turned to AI to generate titles, loading two chapters at a time for a test. Some results:

- The Art of Being Seen
- Living from the Inside Out
- Meeting the Stranger Within
- Unmasking the Self
- Feast on Your Life
- Through the Mirror of Intimacy
- Revealing the Hidden Self
- The Vulnerability of Being
- The Dance of Self and Other

Amazing titles, all. But for different books. The essential element of humor was gone. Inspired by the title of Steve Martin's book *Born Standing Up*, I asked AI to generate titles on the idea of being "… born funny with a spiritual orientation." Results:

- Born With a Divine Sense of Humor
- Blessed With Comedic Insight
- Spiritually Inclined, Naturally Funny
- Comedically Enlightened
- Funny For a Higher Purpose
- Humor With a Spiritual Soul
- Born With a Cosmic Sense of Humor
- Comedic With Higher Consciousness

Interesting. But I wanted a title that not only told readers the book was funny, but was funny in and of itself; I wanted it to make people laugh. So I loaded the entirety of the 43,000-word manuscript with the working title: *Turds of Wisdom! #2!* Instantly, AI responded with something like, "Uh, dude, you already have a title!" Then I loaded in the whole book again, this time trying (and apparently failing) to remove every reference to the working title. Results:

- Wisdom Nuggets (Flush Twice for Clarity)
- Enlightenment in the Bathroom Stall
- Mind Dumps: Volume 2
- Holy Crap: More Thoughts from a Buddhist Rebel
- The Zen of Number Two
- Deep Thoughts from the Porcelain Throne
- Turds of Wisdom: Flushed with Insight
- Turds of Wisdom: The Number Two Edition
- Wisdom Droppings: The Number Two Collection
- Droppings of Genius: Another Pile of Thoughts

OMG! I laughed myself silly. There really seems to be something to this AI! Many of them still crack me up. Next refinement—remove every fragment of every title reference, along with every instance of the word turds. Results:

- The Art of Overthinking (and Other Life Skills)
- Deep Thoughts from the Shallow End
- Zen and the Art of Grin-F*ing
- Laughing in the Face of Enlightenment
- My Life as a Failed Guru
- Half-Baked Wisdom and Totally Baked Ideas
- Enlightenment for Assholes
- Peeing Under Pressure and Other Life Lessons

Loved them all. But what's the point of taking out turds if numerous other words remain to potentially offend? Further refinement was required; I needed to take out any words like *fucking*, *assholes*, and *peeing*. Results:

- Half-Baked Wisdom and Fully Absurd
- Enlightenment for the Deeply Confused
- Laughing All the Way to the Abyss
- The Jester's Guide to Reality
- My Life as a Cosmic Joke
- How Not to Be a Guru

- The Fine Art of Screwing Up
- This Book Will Not Change Your Life

How about that last one? Could be the choice title to cut through all the self-help clutter at your local bookstore. But I still hadn't found The One. Moving parts of titles around like puzzle pieces, recombining them and adding new elements, I brainstormed on my own and came up with these:

- The Failed Guru
- Deep Thoughts, Shallow Pool, Much Absurdity
- Accidentally Wise, Fully Absurd
- My Personal Guarantee: "This Book Will Not Change Your Life"
- No Success—Guaranteed!
- The Anti-Self Help Book
- What I Learned From Failing at Self-Help
- A Jester's Guide to Reality
- Overthinking (And Other Life Skills)
- Half-Baked Wisdom and Fully-Baked Nonsense
- Feast On Your Life: Deep Thoughts From a Cannibal
- Zen and the Art of Malarky
- Peeing Under Pressure: Confessions Of a Sacred Fool

And there it was: *Confessions of a Sacred Fool*. Minus the peeing phrase, this title seemed to capture much of the tone of the book. Though not funny and still requiring the subtitle to better explain the content, I thought it was a title I could live with, especially considering that I knew the cover image could also add humor and meaning. Being exhausted with the entire process by that point helped too.

This book is not a memoir, though there are memoir-like chapters. Nor is it a compilation of essays, though you'll find some mini-essays. It's also not a Buddhist book per se, certainly not a traditional one that deigns to explain dharma principles. Nonetheless, I like to think all the stories are informed by a Buddhist orientation. The book does contain, once again, absurd stories and absurd takes on topics of interest. Nothing is meant to be sequential, either chronologically or thematically. For those things, I recommend a good book.

So feel free to skip around to whatever chapter calls you. Of course, you can read it from front to back since there is a certain logic there. I don't know what that logic is, but my editor tells me it's there somewhere. I view it as a hearkening back to the collage structure of my films from the 1980s—this time with words rather than images. I'm endeavoring to create art rather than anything that fits a standard book format.

But take it slowly. One advance reader told me it's like drinking from a firehose. My recommendation? Don't drink from a firehose! Take small sips, maybe only a chapter at a time. Take in whatever measured amount amuses you or seizes your imagination. Then put it aside. Putting it aside could be the best long-term value the book bestows.

Introduction

IT ALL STARTS WITH REALITY. But what's actually real is surprisingly elusive. Our busy minds make it difficult to know exactly what's real, much less accept it once it is known. We have to fight through all our projections and judgments, all the ways our emotions color what we see and experience, all the ways our history becomes the stories we tell ourselves about our lives. That is a lot of baggage to carry. If we can succeed in putting that baggage down, in opening our eyes and hearts to what's really happening at any moment, then we have the opportunity to discover the infinite wondrous possibilities that the real represents.

To begin we have to do our emotional and psychological work. That means uncovering the wounds of the past—everyone has them dating back to childhood—and uncovering our shadows—those beliefs we took on about ourselves and the world that started with our wounds and now trip us as we aspire to move on. We all have shadows, the dark side, the parts of ourselves we hide, repress, and deny. Until they're made conscious they will continue to undermine our greatest intentions. Our shadows must be fully integrated and yoked to our sense of purpose in life.

The agreements we make, spoken and unspoken, with all those we interact with, constitute the ground on which we walk through life. Without a deep commitment to complete accountability, to living in integrity, matching our words and actions, all relationships, and eventually community and all of society, break down. Commitment to upholding agreements is the glue that holds people together. Love is important, but less important than being accountable to your love, to placing yourself in service to those loves. Being accountable is what makes sustaining community possible.

Regular, intentional rituals are a necessity for marking our journey through life. Through ritual and rites of passage we become acquainted with our life's deepest purpose and remain on track to live it. Most of us engage in some ceremonies—graduations, weddings, birthdays, funerals… But we need more, and we need all of them to carry vastly increased import. They have to mean something to us not only emotionally but psychically. They have to affect us subconsciously, archetypally—at those regions of the self connected to ways of being that are 50,000 years old. We need rituals for ending childhood, for puberty, for leaving home, for becoming an adult man or woman, for preparing to take a spouse or start a family, for becoming elders, for preparing to die. By marking these occasions publicly we reaffirm and solidify community.

Truly grounded in reality, uncolored by stories of the past and mental projections, free of unspoken or unconscious agendas, we can awaken to the endless possibilities of the now. Living in the now becomes an exciting opportunity for growth, for experiencing life in a new way, for acts of compassion, for realignment with what most fulfills us, for creative expression. Free of trying to preserve appearances, of protecting the ego, of "saving face," we can engage more fully and humbly in what the moment asks of us.

We honor our ignorance by learning from other people and other cultures. We listen deeply to discern *what is*. This is what makes life feel full, not rushing about to acquire new things or go new places. But we never shrink from asserting our voice. If we need to teach, we teach. If we need to learn, we become students. We're ready to become both mentor and mentee. In fact, we need to be both. That up/down connection is what anchors us to our lineage, our sense of where we are in time: up by inheriting the wisdom of our ancestors, down by gifting our descendants. By mentoring and being mentored we sustain and perpetuate the values of beloved community.

Spiritual practice provides both the stable ground we walk on and the philosophical framework for all we do. Through meditation and prayer we listen deeply to silence—the wellspring of all wisdom. Spiritual practice reminds us we are all interdependent, that what each of us does impacts countless others. That we take care of each other not out of a sense of obligation or altruism, but because it's how we take care of ourselves. Just as wound and shadow work constitute *soul work*—driving our psychic roots deep into the earth, into the past, into dirt and darkness—spiritual practice constitutes *spirit work*—driving our trunk and branches skyward, into the future, into light and infinite possibility.

The capacity for endless human transformation exists in all of us. We are, each of us, at our greatest depth, good. This is where our Buddha nature, the god within, resides.

> *When each of us lives the purpose in life we were designed for the world will live in perfect harmony.*
> —Buckminster Fuller

Consumption is the pathway to unfulfillment—*dukkha* is the Pali word for it, meaning unsatisfactoriness or suffering. Only giving our gifts freely in service to others can bring deep joy and fulfillment in life.

> *I slept and dreamt that life was joy. I awoke and saw that life was service. I acted and behold, service was joy.*
> —Rabindranath Tagore

Spiritual practice and regular ritual allow us to know and appreciate that death is coming. We don't live in fear of it, or become morbid or despairing; we simply accept its fundamental reality. It will take us all at any moment, ready or not. Once we truly know and accept this we become free, free to rejoice in what we have now.

CHAPTER ONE

Heyokha!

OVER THE LAST 50 YEARS I've referred to myself by many of the following words and phrases: bohemian, shadow watcher, jester, iconoclast, non-conformist, lone wolf, free-thinker, satirist, troublemaker, anti-establishment truth-teller holding a mirror to society, culture, and institutions. At different times and to varying degrees, those terms have been helpful to me but none of them worked to encapsulate who I was at my core. OK, I probably shouldn't overlook *buffoon*, *ass* and *nitwit*. Still, it took sitting my 13th Hollow Bones meditation retreat at the Pine Ridge reservation for me to finally understand who I am. I am Heyokha.

There is no equivalent term in English. Sacred Fool is my nearest favorite. It contains both expansiveness and precision. Part of why no direct translation is possible is because the dual roles Heyokhas play in Lakota society—ceremonially and in everyday life—are unique to their culture. In community life, Heyokhas function similarly to ombudsmen. While there may not be any immediately discernible reason for what Heyokhas do— why ride a horse backward?—they are completely accepted. More than just given a place in the village circle and made to feel welcome, more than just tolerated, in ceremonies they are viewed as bearers of important messages. They bear news that community members know implicitly they need to hear. They speak deep truths, often in ways that are bizarre or funny. They are seen as visionary, as dancers-between-the-worlds. In most of our institutions today, except for arts and entertainment, there is no place for Heyokhas. As Malidoma Somé once said, "If you want to speak your truth, better keep a fast horse by the door."

Though not exactly the same, stop and think for a moment about whistleblowers and how they are treated. 90% are fired from their jobs. Of that number, very few get hired by other companies because corporations only see them as troublemakers. "If they did it once they'll do it again." So, they're effectively blackballed. Federal whistleblowers get fired at 10 times the rate of other workers. Whistleblowers in organized labor typically lose their legal cases 2/3 of the time. The vast majority of people who may revere those who speak truth to power typically have little power and influence themselves. Meanwhile, the full force of the state and/or corporations can be brought to bear against them, not only by firing them, but to subordinate, isolate, smear, threaten, fine, blackmail, imprison, and even kill them.

Fortunately, WikiLeaks founder Julian Assange no longer languishes in a British prison awaiting possible extradition to the US where he was wanted for receiving and spreading classified information—for telling US citizens what the government didn't want them to know. A similar fate awaits Edward Snowden should he be foolhardy enough to re-enter the US. On track for a lifetime of exile in Russia (as long as he is useful to Putin for poking a finger in the eye of the US government), I consider him a hero for exposing the myriad ways the NSA spies on all Americans. You too could be in line for hero status, or martyrdom, as long as you're willing to take the heat from the powers that be for loudly telling the truth.

Though no hero, I have taken the truth-seeker path less traveled. From my earliest days I felt apart, different. By my early teens, I knew that societal paths to success and achievement held no interest for me. I couldn't figure out why people were so anxious to have 2.2 children, a house in the suburbs, and two cars in the garage. (Though having 1/5th of a child does intrigue me.) Raising children, living life in a nuclear family, making money and building a traditional career, even receiving all the standard markers of achievement… none of it held much appeal. Traditional life felt like a form of slavery. This was not something I learned in books and adopted as an ideology; I was born this way. I was born Heyokha.

As with whistleblowers, so with artists. Anyone thinking rationally never becomes an artist. You do it because you have to. No other path is fulfilling or makes sense. You just have to recognize that society does not stand by to shower you with rewards. It's a slog to make a living to support your art and, even with success, fans' expectations can make it hard to sustain. "Shut up and sing!" the Dixie Chicks were told when they opposed President Bush's invasion of Iraq. Fame, money, and power accrue to those who tend not to challenge the status quo too loudly or too often. Ed Asner, the actor who played Lou Grant on *The Mary Tyler Moore Show*, had his own TV show canceled and his career set back for publicly advocating support for El Salvador leftists. I sometimes wonder if Ken Burns would continue receiving support from the Corporation for Public Broadcasting and General Motors if he made films about present-day social issues. It's one thing to highlight issues like racism from the distant past and quite another to talk about its residual life in contemporary power-wielding institutions. It's hard to imagine Michael Moore having the success he's had without his goofball comic persona to help sell his politics. Those are the lucky ones—the ones who succeeded. Most artists, especially if they challenge the social norms, are not in line to receive recognition and acclaim.

God bless those people out there fighting the status quo. But that's not my fight, that's not my calling. If I don't have a reputation for speaking truth to power, it's largely because as an artistic subject it doesn't interest me. Why state the obvious? As Leonard Cohen put it:

> *"Everybody knows the good guys lost*
> *Everybody knows the fight was fixed*
> *The poor stay poor, the rich get rich*
> *That's how it goes*
> *Everybody knows."*

What more need be said? My entire output of books and movies is proof I've gone in a different direction. Heyokha are innovators as much (or more) of form than of content. I like to question the so-called normal way of doing things and try something different. Conventions are just that—conventional. Other than habit, blindly perpetuating the status quo, what makes the normative ways of doing things simpler, cheaper, more efficient, more satisfying or more meaningful? What makes them better? When you drill into those questions, typically the answer is "not much."

Personally, I like to work during most American holidays. When others are busy dutifully fulfilling responsibilities as consumers, I like to hunker down. The phone stops ringing. The cessation of social activity and noise creates a cocoon of quiet. If I have to go out, I like walking empty streets during Christmas or New Year's or Super Bowl Sunday. I always seek to drive during off-peak hours, when few are going my way. No question, privilege allows me this opportunity. Similarly, I'm lucky (and contrary) enough to take time off when everyone else is working. I'm able to take "vacations" any day at any time by meditating, swimming, sitting in the hot tub, extending a lunch date to two hours, or by reading books and watching movies as part of my research. During COVID-19, I often rode my bike to the San Francisco Bay to sit on a park bench across from Alameda Island to read or work on my laptop. I don't vacation much anymore per se, but I enjoy work so much it feels like vacation, especially when I get to take work-related travel.

When making plans to watch movies with others, I'm also contrary. I tell people up front that I'm a snob. I don't have much patience for the latest Hollywood releases—the comic books, video games, and branded toys passed off as movies. Well-versed in the four principal modes of cinema creation—documentary, fiction, animation, and experimental, along with their various hybrids—it's painfully clear to me that what is popular is usually a far cry from art. The TV series that get attention on streaming services leave me cold, no matter how many proliferate. Their subject matter might be cutting edge with great actors and directors, but most seem to be glorified soap operas.

The questions I ask myself: Does the film help you see the world in a new way? Do you feel altered or changed in ways you couldn't begin to articulate? Do you feel a physical impact somewhere in your body, like how standing on the prairie must once have felt with the pounding of a million stampeding buffalo? Questions like these lead me to the answers I seek. That's what art does. Do I drive my girlfriend crazy when it comes time to curl up together on the couch to watch an evening flick? Of course! Same with most of my friends. That's why I started my Sunday Night Cinema Club. When we invite people over to the house to watch a movie, they understand they're subjecting themselves to my tastes. I choose the fare. God help those who don't have the stomach for motion picture art. It usually means naptime for my girlfriend.

When someone says to me, "You've got to see this"—be it a movie, a selfie, a news story, a TikTok meme—I pause. Why? Just because everyone else is? Sometimes I wonder if they really know me. For the last ten years I've paid to have someone manage our different Warrior Films social media accounts, partly because I'm tired of defending my position that all forms of social media are largely a waste of time. Yes, I'd rather pay someone to do it for me than explain yet again how useless it can be. My friend Larry, who at last count had close to 3 million followers on Facebook, said it best when he told me that his support was miles wide and not an inch deep. A master at training dogs, he can't get more than a handful of those 3 million to buy his dog training books. I accept that the things I do might be of interest to some people, whether it's film-related activities or sharing occasional mind wanderings, but the thought of filling people in on my everyday goings-on fills me with nausea. The biggest lie social media has sold us is that everything we do is somehow fascinating. Sorry, it's not. I'm not and you're not. Will someone please invent a vaccine for the disease "Everyone's a Star?" (Maybe they already have and it's called real life.) Even if my greatest heroes were to engage in regular social media shares, I can't imagine taking the slightest interest. "I had the most delicious piece of salmon for dinner last night." Bob Dylan. "Does anyone know of a good non-toxic weed killer?" Steph Curry. "I finally retired my favorite flannel shirt and bought a new one." Bernie Sanders. "I switched my go-to coffee bean from Koa to Arabica." Patti Smith. Amazing, world-changing talents, every one, but the details of their personal lives—who cares? What could be duller?

Once again, that perspective puts me in the minority. On websites like OnlyFans.com the world's voyeurs now line up to pay people to watch them bathe their feet, prepare a meal, clip their nails, and feed the cat. We're not talking celebrities. These are everyday people. Apparently, fetishes come in many varieties. These John Does might be well on their way to stardom, but I guess it depends on how sexily they brush their teeth. Though it excites me to think I could actually earn money from allowing people to watch me meditate, inject insulin, stretch my neck, make potato salad, charge my Chevy Bolt, or swim, I'm not sure I'm ready for that level of intrusion.

"What?" you may say. "Au contraire! You already do nothing *but* expose yourself!" That's true. In my early films and in my recent books—take this one as Exhibit C—I share countless details about my own life. Even intimate details. But for me, the discriminating factor is having it serve a valuable purpose. I do it only after serious reflection and only with the most selective intentions: to induce empathy, to encourage or inspire, to open hearts and minds, to gift laughter or cause reflection. I'm not offering undigested pabulum for voyeuristic consumption. With all my films and books I want to motivate people to think for themselves, to reconsider their own lives and choices. I want to create art, not sensation. I don't always succeed, but I try. Heyokhas are discerning!

Leo Lionni's children's book, *Frederick,* is one of my all-time favorites. My college girlfriend gave me a copy for my 22nd birthday. It deftly inverts Aesop's classic fable *The Ant and the Grasshopper* that celebrates the Protestant work ethic. In that story Grasshopper plays music all summer while the ants work on the grain harvest. When winter comes and Grasshopper asks for food, the ants give him the cold shoulder, presumably consigning him to starvation for skirting his share of the work. "He had his chance!" they say. Now he must suffer.

Frederick, a mouse, appears very much like our fabled grasshopper. While the other mice are busy working to prepare for the winter, Frederick is out collecting the smells, sights, and sounds of summer. This time everyone runs out of food in the winter, the mice too, so Frederick steps in by recounting those same smells, sights, and sounds from summer. Transforming his experiences into art, he fills their minds with visions, with poetry, quieting their hunger and feeding their souls. From this simple inversion of society's values, I take lasting inspiration. The notion that my gifts to community lie not in traditional labor but in storytelling and the arts was a revelation for me. I'm not useless, some grasshopper sponge trying to soak surplus out of the economy, or to use the slanderous, right-wing term, some "welfare queen." I am, in fact, a powerful contributor to society, offering gifts of another order. It never hurt that the star mouse was also my namesake. Frederick is Heyokha.

My Zen teacher—Junpo Denis Kelly—was Heyokha. A large part of why I was drawn to the Hollow Bones Zen order was through the man himself. When I met him I recognized a kindred spirit. I loved the Dharma, and he was certainly an excellent teacher. But I had never before experienced a teacher who embodied what the Tibetans call *crazy wisdom*. Certainly, Chögyam Trungpa Rinpoche fit this mode. Maybe Bernie Glassman of the Zen Peacemakers order did too. Junpo was the embodiment of crazy wisdom. Whether due to his nature from birth, or due to the massive amounts of LSD he consumed in his formative years, Junpo knew the three marks of existence in his own hollow bones: impermanence (*anicca*), suffering (*dukha*), and no-self (*anatta*). Living life from a deep comprehension of those truths can make everyday goings-on pretty amusing. I recommend seeking out people like that. They're often a lot of fun to be around.

Since Junpo died in 2021, I've been wrestling with where I fit into the order he founded. None of the present-day roshis and teachers seem to embody crazy wisdom. Which is not to take anything away from them, they're all wonderful teachers and fine human beings in their unique ways. But I have reservations about how far their insight and wisdom actually go. Certainly as an institution, Hollow Bones, as fledgling as it is, itself on the cusp of renewal, lacks the edgy quality of Heyokha—welcoming extreme difference and divergence, welcoming unwelcome news. Driven by my nature, I see no other way forward than, once again, charting my own path to become a barefoot Boddhisattva, or as Zen Master Tōrei Enji put it, *a Boddhisattva of no rank*, wandering my way through life, sharing teachings in all the momentary ways that arise—some downright crazy—without an institution to call home, laughing as I go.

In 1988, my first full year practicing and studying Buddhism, I saw this future in an epiphany. Chanting the sutras one day I suddenly saw myself in old age. In that vision I spent most of my time spreading and teaching the Dharma. I was a respected man of the community and had many students. Now that I'm 69 I'd like to realize that vision. Old age is here. I'm a somewhat respected man of the community. Though I don't have any students, why should that stop me? Time for this Heyokha to hit the trail, leaving *Confessions of a Sacred Fool* in my wake.

CHAPTER TWO

Being Evil

I REMEMBER MY MOTHER driving my older sister and me to high school one day. I was probably 14. I was making the point that if/when I ever had kids I'd never teach them euphemisms for body functions. Forget "peeing" and "pooping." Forget "number 1 or number 2." My parents taught us, "ah-ah or pee-pee?" Talk about humiliating. I can't stand talking down to kids. I'd say, "Time for a piss, Suzy? Bobby, need to take a shit?" Those were the terms I used for myself and would be the words I'd use for my kids. Mom and sis then went on to tell me how when I became an adult, I'd also outgrow my teenage tendency to use swear words. My not unreasoned response was "Fuck you! I like swearing now and I'm still going to fucking like it when I'm 60!" I offer this story as sufficient proof that it has come to pass.

Being the rational sort, I often wonder if I should become evil. It's certainly not without its benefits. Look around: many of the world's leaders informally compete for Evil-Doer of the Month. If only they would have a contest to determine who will be Evil-Doer of the Year; the winner would have to kill all the others, doing us all a modified public service.

The rewards of evil-doing are many and varied, especially if you're of the billionaire variety: wealth, power, privilege, fame, sex, hobnobbing with celebrities, homes in the Bahamas, never taking out the trash…

There are outliers of course. I was encouraged when the playwright Vaclav Havel, having spent much of his life in communist prisons, was elected President of Czechoslovakia after the 1990 Velvet Revolution. Prime Minister Jacinda Ardern of New Zealand struck me as very capable and just, until she was hounded out of office. Maia Sandu is doing heroic things to keep her little country of Moldova from falling into Russian hands. I read an article about Leah Hunt-Hendrix, one of the heiresses to the Hunt oil fortune in Texas. She certainly seems to be doing a lot of wonderful things with her money, primarily fighting climate change, which of course her own family and fortune helped create. Guilt can be a wonderful motivator!

Certainly the vast majority of good guys have been murdered in their tracks. The journalist Jamal Khashoggi comes immediately to mind—murdered in the Saudi consulate in Istanbul by agents of his own government. "Welcome! Keep right for passport renewal and visas. Keep left for torture and dismemberment." As far as I know, Wikipedia doesn't keep a running tally of Unsung Heroes. Maybe that's fortunate. The list would run hundreds of pages long and be a reading exercise of excruciating proportions.

Thank goodness doing good is never necessary since being evil is always an option. It comes down to practicalities. A five-decade study was recently completed in England which determined that aggression at school led to better paying jobs. Bullies succeeded more regularly than the emotionally insecure, eventually becoming higher earners. Professor Emilia Del Bono, one of the study's authors, said, "It's possible that our classrooms are competitive places and that children adapt to win that competition with aggression, and then take that through to the workplace where they continue to compete aggressively for the best-paid jobs. Perhaps we need to reconsider discipline in schools and help to channel this characteristic in children in a more positive way." Ya think?

In 1986 when Ivan Boesky famously said that greed is healthy, he was an outlier. Today it's the cultural norm. When systems are rotten, you either adapt to the going rules or consign yourself to oblivion. Somebody could help you with groceries, let's say, and you'd walk away thinking, *Loser*. I never subscribed to Dr. Martin Luther King Jr.'s contention that "the arc of the moral universe is long, but it bends toward justice." I subscribe more to the maxim: "There's no telling what life might serve up. But if it's justice you're looking for, good luck!" Today it's dog eat dog, winner take all. These are the sweepstakes of late capitalism, the ethos. Accepting this can prove comforting.

Doing good is time-consuming and the pay sucks. I want to get on with it, get things done, not sit around shooting the shit. Can we just be transactional please and forget being relational? They're separate worlds: the world of business and the world of relationships. In the world of business (and, frankly, art) it's boom, boom, boom, get to the point, make it happen and move on. (Which is why it's taking me page after page to explain this.) This is my experience with the rich and famous. Wealthy people rarely begin with niceties. It's all business. Backstage after a play, John Malkovich appeared out of nowhere, said nothing by way of introduction, and started talking to me about Chicago high school basketball. He knew I was famous for Hoop Dreams, so he launched right in. I aspire to be like Werner Herzog—doing whatever it takes to get films made. It doesn't necessarily mean doing evil but it can come close. He's come very close. Most studies indicate that people would commit crimes if they knew they could get away with them. I'm sick to death of hearing "Do the right thing!" which was my mother's mantra to me. It's an admonition, not an invitation. I don't want to be schooled; I want to be inspired. Does *anyone* want to be told "be nice"? Many derivations of *nice* conflate with inauthenticity. Some days I just want to run over a kid on his bicycle.

My graduate school girlfriend Beth once said something wise. At the time, I was distraught about all the dark thoughts I was having. She said, "You're a creative. Of course you're going to have thoughts like that. Not every thought you have is going to be goodness and light. Don't worry about it." I immediately relaxed and happily resumed plotting to kill my department chair.

The Christian system is pristine and simple. Sign, give away your soul, and get shit done. Clear, clean, transactional. I can only imagine how successful and famous I'd get. Working with the devil the hours are good and there's plenty of room for advancement. But after 69 years of searching, I can't find the devil. At least not outside myself.

Buddhism is less clear-cut. The law of karma, otherwise known as the law of cause and effect, is simple enough. Do something nefarious and you'll pay the price. What makes the law confounding is that it's not a one-to-one relationship. There's no eye for an eye. Steal somebody's lawnmower and it may not mean that someone will steal yours, or that the lawnmower itself will eventually run over your foot. What Buddhist teachings indicate is that the repercussions of your action could cause untold suffering for yourself and others. You may feel guilty about it. It may unleash a string of increasingly elaborate lies to tell your family where it came from, leading to a loss of trust which could end with the kids acting out or your spouse wanting a divorce. The key word is *untold*. You don't know how bad it might be or how long it might take. You just have to wait and see what happens. You may not go to Christian Hell, but you could end up in a living hell. Just ask Raskolnikov from *Crime and Punishment*. Though his timeline of comeuppance was pretty short, he certainly carried a lot of hurt for his crime of murder. I consider him a soul-brother.

I'm still waiting for some of the people who screwed me to get their comeuppance. I'm impatient and would like to know, where is their karma? It's the Christmas package that never arrives. That's partly how I've created a living hell for myself. Sitting around waiting for fate to serve up revenge on all your foes is not conducive to happiness.

Yet evil perpetually beckons. Clearly, being a good person is getting me nowhere. Maybe it's time to stop the high-road bullshit and try something different. Maybe it's time to fake my own death so interest in my work will skyrocket. Maybe it's time to lie and say President Obama wrote me a book blurb: "I wish I'd known Frederick Marx's work while still in office. It might have significantly helped my peace efforts throughout the world." Maybe it's time to steal valor and pass myself off as a Veteran, or use a pseudonym and pretend I'm a black woman making her first film. Maybe it's time to imitate Morgan Freeman's voice for my documentary film narration. Or maybe it's time to leave a long note listing all my betrayals and disappointments, give every last shit-heel a final fuck you, and kill myself. Think of it as the lighter side of suicidal ideation.

The film business exacerbates this. I'm sure there are a few people in Hollywood at the very top who've always taken the high road. But who can say? Why not join what seems like the status quo and try lying, backstabbing, and cheating? It could be a refreshing change of pace. As Megan McArdle put it in a recent op-ed in *The Daily Beast*: "Sometimes you must leave the high road and fetch your brass knuckles." My former Hoop Dreams partners could qualify as recipients. For over 30 years they've systematically deprived me of receiving equal recognition for the work I did on the film. It continues to this day, and it's impossible to gauge how this has adversely affected my career.

For a few weeks I worked for Bahman Ghobadi on his film *Turtles Can Fly*. In the early aughts, he was a darling of the international cinema scene. Looking through the dailies one day, I was shocked to see him slap one of his child actors, a five-year-old boy, to get him to cry on camera. Standards are certainly different in Iran than the US. Yet, even with a high pressure shoot costing thousands of dollars a day, this wasn't corporal punishment; the kid did nothing wrong. He just didn't perform on cue. I'm not sure I could go that far.

That's my problem. I can't seem to overcome my inhibitions and get the experience I need to become an evil-doer. There must be a waiting list somewhere for a course on the dark web: "Dispense with the Niceties and Murder Your Way to Success." I need a mentor. Where is that evil son of a bitch willing to shine the light forward? Who will open their heart to me and come clean with all the despicable things they've done to become successful? I know some prosperous Hollywood producers who, by most accounts, are loathsome assholes. Maybe they would hire me so I could observe step by painstaking step how shitty behavior leads to success. Certainly Roy Cohn as depicted in the recent film *The Apprentice* serves as a model. Maybe I'll post a want ad in the *Hollywood Reporter*. "Needed immediately: Really vile Hollywood figure to serve as guide. Must be successful. Age and gender need not matter. Must have well established history of wretched behavior. References welcome from the maimed or tortured."

But we shouldn't look at this through rose-colored glasses. There are downsides to doing evil. For one it's a lot of trouble. Even our system of justice—the best that money can buy—is not foolproof. Even though the Supreme Court has decided the president is above the law, all the money in the world might fail you and you could find yourself serving time, like Ivan Boesky, Jeffrey Epstein, or Martha Stewart. Getting re-elected was certainly the best Get Out of Jail Free card Trump could have devised. But lying is not easy. Just remembering lies is taxing. I'm lazy. I prefer simplicity. Lies get complicated and typically involve drama. Who wants all that complication and drama? I may be an undervalued artist but at least I'm not busy. If you always speak the truth then you never need concern yourself with what's important to remember. The world around me offers up quite enough drama, thank you. Referencing people's propensity to create drama, Alan Watts once quoted an old Zen saying: "You're trying to create ocean waves when there's no wind present." That could be me. Better to float along and wait for the breeze. Doing evil requires heavy rowing.

Once you decide you're not cut out for evil, there's really no other direction to turn. You're stuck on the course of goodness with no possible recourse. It's terrible. You have to give up strategies of tricking or bullying people and accept that the only option left is to be kind and hope they'll respond, well, in kind. Yes, it can cause frustration; it's terribly constricting. Nobody likes to have their options limited, certainly not me. But if someone disappoints or betrays you, you no longer have the latitude of going off on them. If someone promises money or an important opportunity and never delivers, you're screwed. You just have to give up and resign yourself to thanking them anyway for their time and interest. It's a failure of sorts. But what is maturity if not accepting failure?

My mother once referred to herself as "a foot soldier of the good." What a wonderful characterization! Struck by its simplicity and power, the only issue I took with her was her lack of ambition. I wanted to be a general of the good! I want to lead, not follow. This conversation took place in the immediate wake of Hoop Dreams' success. I had grand plans for the films I wanted to make in Hollywood and for the splendid home I was going to live in after I made my first million. She was generous with her lack of judgment, though I remember her saying, "I don't know about a million dollars." Having more sense than me was only one of her many virtues. Assuming I'd eventually stop swearing wasn't one of them. Now, in her honor, I'm going to stop fucking around and go ah-ah.

CHAPTER THREE

At Sea

TRAVEL! SO EXCITING! You get to see the world, have adventures, and get thrown in jail.

I was 22 when I experienced all three on an around-the-world voyage. Or, what should have been an around-the-world voyage. I only made it part way. The ship was called World Campus Afloat, and managed by Chapman College from 1965–1975. But the program got sold to the University of Colorado. I enrolled for the spring semester, 1977, when it was reborn and rebranded Semester at Sea. That could be the moral of this story—beware rebrandings! Caveat emptor!

The S.S. Universe sailed out of LA in early February 1977, scheduled to dock over three months later in New York. It was to be my final college semester, affording me the transferable credits I needed to complete my BA at the University of Illinois. I could finish college and have a great adventure at the same time. It was four years earlier, sitting on a Moroccan beach in a hashish daze with an alum that I first heard about it. "Want to join a floating party filled with interesting faculty cruising around the world?" Is this a trick question? In later years, Bishop Tutu, Fidel Castro, Mikhail Gorbachev, Mother Teresa, Arthur C. Clarke and other notables sailed part way with the ship or offered onboard presentations. Who says no to that?

"This is not a floating party!" were pretty much the first words I heard when I came aboard. The brand-new administrators and faculty from the University of Colorado were hell bent on changing the ship's reputation. No Southern California laissez-faire attitude to drugs was to be tolerated. I can't say I was particularly concerned. That lack of concern didn't take long to manifest as disaster.

Sailing to Hawaii afforded us time to familiarize ourselves with onboard life. I was introduced to yoga. Learning to do a shoulder stand on a slippery tile floor while the ship was rocking made it easy to manage later on dry land. You had to be careful diving into the pool because the water at the deep end wasn't always there when you arrived. My two roommates were likable enough, but I deemed them too square to spend time with. It might have been one of them who later ratted me out.

We formed a small circle—me, and a few oddballs and misfits. In a vote that never took place, it seems I was elected chairman. I might have been the oldest. I certainly was the tallest and cheekiest. Smoking pot in an alcove above the bow one breezy night I had a flash of insight into mind control: "These three people would do anything I wanted." They were in thrall to my charisma. I resolved then and there never to assume any position of leadership whatsoever because it could lead to acting out unsavory impulses. Given my immaturity at the time this was a healthy instinct. My concern might've been enhanced by a horoscope reading from an amateur astrologer who once told me I could become one of the world's most evil people. That would have been especially bad form in the 1970s. Like many college students, I was obsessed with anti-authoritarian structures, so it was wise to take preventative action. This was before I was introduced to Jung's concept of the human shadow and learned how everyone harbors their own little dictators. Though I never acted out this particular shadow—the idea of becoming isolated with adoring supplicants fills me with dread—it took me over 20 years to finally dispel the nonsense that leadership, in and of itself, is harmful.

I became friends with two people younger than me who eventually paid a steep price for their loyalty. The woman I'll call Jennifer hailed from the Boston area. I can't remember where the other one, who I'll call Max, was from, so I'll make up that he was from Oklahoma. He had a kind of down-home charm.

I brought along my recently purchased Panasonic Portapak—one of the earliest home video recorders. It recorded in black and white and was connected to the camera by an umbilical cable. Typically slung over the shoulder with a strap, my prize possession weighed about 20 pounds. "Guerilla video," we called it. We were confident it would usher in the information utopia where every citizen would become a creator of the news. Not quite 50 years later I'd say that revolution has arrived, and it looks like dystopia to me. With my sociology professor's approval, in lieu of a final paper, I determined to submit my trip report on video. Measured against my later oeuvre it likely would've been shit, but it would have constituted my first documentary.

Oahu was our initial port of call. We toured Pearl Harbor and the memorials for the hundreds of seamen who had been lost. I was shocked to see the ships so near the dock sitting in just a few feet of water. When we crossed the International Date Line, I organized a search party to find the missing day. You could say that I approached the trip as a joke. More than carefree, I felt liberated. The whole world was mine.

We initially limited pot smoking to the upper deck, out in the open air, in the dark. But I grew incautious. Three days sail out of Hawaii I decided it was safe to smoke in my cabin. I was later told that the fumes were recognizable the entire length of the deck. The fateful knock came soon enough, and a search party burst into the room. Present were the director of student admissions and the man I later came to think of as my primary nemesis, the resident enforcer from the University of Colorado, the man who proclaimed: "This is not a floating party." I don't recall what anyone said in the way of a greeting or if it was even possible to refuse them entry. They searched the room. Pot seemed to be their sole objective. I remember screaming a silent prayer while the Enforcer made his way through the drawers of my desk. "Please, please, please don't find the LSD!" Never one to succeed at poker, I stared directly down into my drawer at a small bag with some scattered pills as the Enforcer rifled through it. How he missed them I'll never understand. But it didn't matter because they found a small amount of pot. I believe it was sitting in plain view in the ashtray with the roach.

The following day I was called into a meeting with the academic brass. Unpleasant would be a fair characterization. They needed an example of their hardline seriousness, and I was the first available candidate. I arrived with my video camera, recording everything. I thought it would serve as a punishment deterrent and, if it came to that, as a valuable record for my defense. Maybe they wouldn't be so severe? The camera probably pissed them off more. I remember the Enforcer fixing me with his assassin's gaze, saying, "You got me in focus?! You're off this ship buddy!" At least I was his buddy. I remember discomfort on the part of the others present, unable or unwilling to challenge the policy or the less than dispassionate behavior of the Enforcer himself. What's really sad? I erased the tape when I sold my portapack some years later. Consider it a misguided manifestation of my unconscious need to move past the experience. Too bad. Given what little it takes for success in the online world today that single moment could well go viral and be recognized as my greatest filmmaking achievement.

Two days later, I made ready to disembark in Busan, South Korea. I had no choice. You want adventure? Be careful what you ask for! I guess I should've been relieved they didn't put me off in North Korea. The night before I had a rich and meaningful discussion with a thoughtful, nerdy guy from my philosophy class about Martin Buber's book *I and Thou*. He was disappointed to learn that I'd soon be kicked off the ship. That made two of us.

They escorted me off to ensure that going through immigration involved more than the perfunctory three-day tourist visa. Too disconnected from my own feelings, I couldn't absorb the shock, fear, and anger. My backpack heavy I trudged through the rain, perplexed about where to go until I happened on a tourist bureau. Delighted to find an attractive young clerk who spoke English, I complained about the weather. She told me it had been dry for months and the rain was welcome respite from the drought. In an instant she flipped my confusion and misery on its head. Welcome to Asia! Another important lesson on the limits of subjectivity, on what an elusive beast "objective reality" is. I and Thou indeed! I asked her for a youth hostel recommendation, so she steered me to a cheap hotel. Futons—years before they became the fixture of every college student's dorm room—were firm and perfect for me, enclosed in wooden frames on the floor. Under a heavy quilt, somehow the coldness of the room felt familiar.

I fell into sightseeing with Jennifer. I had no immediate plans; why not enjoy her company while I could? In port for a few more nights, we visited the ancient capital city of Gwangju, ate large amounts of street vendor bulgogi and drank weak Korean beer.

Having touristed in Turkey in my teens, I knew that if I could get to India I could travel overland very cheaply all the way back to Europe. The Magic Bus! Calcutta to London for $250! I had $847 to my name that I'd scrimped from my weekend job as a film projectionist and, OK, a few small-scale drug deals on the side. But how to get to India? The cheapest and most direct route was through China and Tibet to Nepal—a very rough 3,000 miles by bus and train. But think of the savings! Nonetheless, China was still effectively closed to the outside world, just starting to shake off the malevolent ghosts of the Cultural Revolution. The great reformer Deng Xiao-Ping didn't take the reins of power until December 1978; I was a year early. Had I had the courage to try to enter through Hong Kong they might've let me in but it's doubtful. The concept of the individual tourist was anathema to communist authorities. You either came, traveled, (and were watched) in a big group or you didn't come at all. And so it remained even in 1983, when I arrived to work and live there full time. Back in 1977, they likely would've considered me a spy. Regardless, I first had to figure out how I could even get there.

At $700, I couldn't afford the one-way flight to Hong Kong. The South China Sea was a massive ocean wall blocking my access to Asia. Three years after the fall of Saigon, Americans were non-starters in Vietnam, Laos and Cambodia. The American government pretty well succeeded in getting the welcome mats rolled up. Somehow I had to round the China Sea into the Malacca Strait and get at least as far as Singapore. It didn't occur to me to pay for travel on a steamship. So I did the next logical thing and tried to get work on a freighter to Calcutta. It would be the fulfillment of a childhood dream to become a merchant seaman. Maybe it was an unconscious desire to emulate my father's wartime service as a Navy midshipman. Back in Busan, I went down to the harbor and looked for work. The clerk in the very first office I walked into kindly explained to me that most of the cargo ships headed south were only a half day's sail out of Japan, already fully crewed by the time they berthed in Korea.

My options were few and dwindling. So I made what seemed the next most logical decision and stowed away onboard the S.S. Universe. At least that would get me to Taiwan. Long after we docked, I thought I could slip off the ship late at night, feign drunkenness, and then go through immigration. How being in Taiwan would significantly improve my prospects of overland travel to Europe wasn't clear but it was a lot closer to Hong Kong than Korea was. Once I got there, I thought other options might open up.

Jennifer and Max convinced me it'd be easy to sneak back onboard ship. We waited until well into the evening the night before departure. There was a sleepy ship's attendant manning the door at the top of the gangplank, not even checking documents. If he paid attention at all he was probably only listening for American accents. Someone took my backpack in advance, so we'd look all the more like a couple kids returning from a rambunctious night on the town.

I went straight to Max's room where I spent the next two days. He didn't have a roommate so there was a spare bunk and, relatively speaking, plenty of room. I spent the time reading. We tried to keep a low profile, so I don't think I visited with anyone other than Max and Jennifer who brought me meals from the dining room. Turns out, that's all it took. They were being watched.

A day out of Keelung Harbor, Fateful Knock #2 came. This time the search party included officers from the ship. I was hustled down into the ship's bowels, through labyrinthine hallways past the engine room to the brig. The brig! Who would've imagined they had one! Does every ship come with one? Is this the industry standard? It opens new frontiers of possibility for university academic discipline. "No, this won't affect your GPA but you're doing two weeks in the brig."

I had crossed over the comparatively safe ground of university administration dealing with a troublesome student and entered the new territory of maritime law dealing with a stowaway. A violation of international law; the ship's captain now decided my fate. The only time I'd seen him was on the first day when the university and ship's staff were introduced. I don't believe he was a US citizen. Regardless, US laws and conventions were not his concern.

Following the pattern established in Busan, Max and Jennifer were kicked off the ship in Keelung Harbor, outside Taipei. I never saw or heard from Max again. He paid a steep price for his loyalty and generosity. In his memory, the only thing I carry with me is shame. I wish I could say I also never saw Jennifer again. Unfortunately, I had the bad sense to show up at her family house in Massachusetts the following summer for a visit with my girlfriend in tow. If I hadn't already given her enough reason to regret her relationship with me, however platonic, that likely cinched it. Like all mothers, Jennifer's mom was sympathetic to our tale, but out of earshot I hope she talked some sense into her daughter. "Caring for that guy took you down. You're well rid of him."

The brig was basically a locked closet piled high with thin, well-worn mattresses of uncertain origin. I tried not to look too closely at the stains, some of which had to have been urine. No sheets, blankets, pillows or toilet. Let's say the air was fragrant. There was no on/off switch for the overhead light. Blazing brightness, night and day, was just part of the decor. Was I on suicide watch? There was no video camera affixed to the ceiling. Since the bulb was sealed in fine wire mesh making it impossible to unscrew, it precluded any attempt I might make to electrocute myself. Did I mention the room was padded? Was it common for merchant marines to go mad and try to hurt themselves? I can't recall much of my thinking but I'm pretty sure committing suicide was not on the list, though pounding the walls to release my feelings might have proven beneficial.

The entire space was 6x8 feet. I know because I walked those eight narrow feet between the mattresses and the padded wall many times. Fortunately the ceiling was seven feet, so I could stand up straight. Luxuriating in seven full inches of head room, without a thing to read, I spent a lot of time looking out the bars of the door's little window into the dim light of the ship's entrails. Though technically a cruise ship, this was no outer berth with an ocean view; there were no windows, not even portholes in the bulkhead. For 36 hours the ship's crew left me there.

Somehow my friend Jeff found me. Having gotten wind of events, he played sleuth and tracked me to the brig. He's the one who told me Max and Jennifer had themselves become refugees. Too bad I wasn't there to document the Enforcer spewing venom at them. When I told Jeff they left me with nothing to eat or drink he disappeared for half an hour and came back with a can of Coors and some peanut butter crackers. His visit buoyed my spirits and provided the added value of affording me a can to pee in. Looking back now with my 69-year-old bladder, it's impossible for me to imagine that I once peed a single time in a 36-hour period into a 12-ounce can. Of the many losses to be mourned through perfect hindsight, my younger bladder is right up there.

Finally, on the morning of the third day, long after the ship had docked, three people came to my cell: the head of student life and two Chinese harbor police. The head of student life explained that I basically had two choices: I could stand trial for illegally entering the country or I could fly directly back to the United States. He helpfully added that since Taiwan was technically still at war with mainland China, trying to enter the country illegally was tantamount to espionage. Accordingly, I would be put on trial as a spy.

There's nothing like a bracing truth to restore you to clarity. I knew, from reading about international human rights that, dating back to the 1948 takeover of Taiwan by Chang Kai-shek, Taiwanese prisons were really bad places to be. Chang ruled the breakaway province as a US supported dictator until his death in 1975, so the practice of mirroring their mainland cousins with brutal anti-democratic policies was well established by the time I came along. Door #2 please!

They gathered all my things from Max's cabin and escorted me off the ship. It felt good to walk around and breathe fresh air. We took the officer's car to the harbor police headquarters where endless rounds of paperwork began. I sat by his desk the whole time while he circulated from post to post talking with colleagues and securing signatures. Though it took hours, I don't recall reading a book or getting bored. Hey, I was in China! OK, I was in a police station, but I was out of the brig! The world was vibrant and alive; everything was of interest.

Documents all stamped, signed, and sealed, it was time to get to the airport. But what flight? My warder secured the services of a travel agent to talk it over. I'm sure it was a wonderful conversation, but I wasn't included. I previously told the officer I wanted to fly to Chicago. Since I only had $815 left, that night's flight to LA was the destination they decided on for me. "Hey, just get him out of here! Who cares where as long as it's to US soil." As an indigent I would be the US government's problem. I later learned that the agent himself coughed up an additional $22 for my ticket. Just when you think it's safe to judge someone harshly, they turn around and betray you with kindness. Foiled again. But what to do until departure?

My handler and the travel agent decided that a late lunch was in order. And so it was that I sat down to the best Chinese buffet ever with the harbor policeman, the travel agent, and two unnamed businessmen at a large and busy restaurant downtown Taipei. I was especially proud of using chopsticks to pick up single peanuts from the bowl rolling by on the lazy susan. Hardly having eaten in two days helped my motivation. They chatted amiably among themselves, occasionally extending open glances in my direction. I knew they were talking about me. How not? If anyone spoke any broken English like my handler, they didn't let on. This was five years before I learned rudimentary Mandarin on the mainland, so I had no clue what they were saying. What I imagined? "Seems a little too compliant to be a spy to me. Maybe he's retarded. For a Big Nose he's reasonably adept with chopsticks." Who the hell cared? I was scarfing delicious Fujian food. I couldn't have named half the dishes but the portions were plentiful, and I relished every bite.

For the drive to the airport I pasted my face to the window. Like a dead man walking, I wanted to get everything I could out of my first, and, as it turned out, last experience of Taiwan. The ship sailing on without me was not remotely on my mind. After the brig, I was suitably chastened, not at all disappointed to be going home.

My keeper, whose name I never properly learned, (maybe I was never told, certainly I never asked), escorted me down the jetway. No last-minute escape was going to be tolerated. I was glad I wasn't in handcuffs so other passengers wouldn't see me getting unshackled. At the door of the plane he shook my hand, looked me in the eye, and said, "When I hear about you I think 'very bad man.' Now I meet you I think 'good man.' I confuse." He promptly turned and walked away.

I was floored. Struck dumb, I watched him go. Talk about shock. But he touched my heart. Even if I had a deep self-awareness back then, I don't think it would've helped matters to sputter, "I'm sorry. I'm just a naive American teen lost in an adult's body desperately seeking initiation into mature manhood. Can you help me? Can you forgive me?"

A "good man?" His images of criminals were likely formed by movies and propaganda—Communist spies, ruthless smugglers, masters of disguise. Not me. The history of my life was pushing the boundaries of acceptable behavior until serious repercussions appeared on the horizon. As troublemakers go, I was milquetoast. Of course I was compliant. I saw no other choice. What was I going to do? Make a run for it when we walked into the restaurant? Throw hot soup at my captors, grab a chopstick from the table and hold it to the waiter's throat demanding safe passage to India? It wasn't like I was a real spy and could make my way through underground Taiwanese society, forging documents and commandeering motorcycles to the coast where I could bribe a fishing trawler to ferry me to Hong Kong. I was a 22-year-old kid who didn't know his ass from a hole in the ground. I wanted to get the hell out of there. I knew the airline food would be decent; I could watch movies and get plenty of free booze. On what I thought would be my last trip ever to Asia, I wanted to make every one of my hard-earned I'm-going-around-the-world dollars count. I bounced a check to fly from LA to Chicago and arrived back home one month to the day after I had left.

If this was the comeuppance I needed to begin to whittle away my adolescent hubris, I can't say with confidence that it succeeded. For a few years, I told this story to entertain friends and win over strangers. It impressed people at parties. Flaunting one's stupidity can provide passing amusement for others. If it didn't, this book wouldn't exist. Then I grew out of it and hardly spoke about it for 45 years. Unless hubris appears in some digested form it really only does a disservice to the teller. Why does arrogance only become clear in hindsight? In the wake of my return, every telling of the story kept the trauma alive, refreshing my shock and despair. PTSD. I kept masking it all as bravado. Finally, I had enough sense to shut the fuck up, to try to retain some dignity until I could bring it to some meaningful terms.

Truth be told, there's still some part of me that longs for adventure on the high seas. And, only five years later, I did move to China for two years, maybe unconsciously finishing unfinished business. But I've still never had that single round-the-world trip. Maybe I'll apply for a job as faculty on the next voyage. After all, I'm an alum. Maybe it'll give me an edge. I can prepare by saying "This is not a floating party."

CHAPTER FOUR

Trying to Pee While a Nurse is Watching

I WAS 14, IN THE HOSPITAL for emergency surgery after my right arm was sliced open. Never play ball tag unsupervised. Chased by the "it" guy with the ball, I was running down a narrow passage between my friend's suburban house and his neighbor's. I thought I'd cut through the side door of the garage and make a clean getaway. Just as I reached for the inset glass window to push the door aside, my friend David, lying in wait, slammed it shut. Good move David! I was definitely "it" now! I looked down and thought, "Oh, there's the inside of my right arm." The skin was gone. Sliced the artery, nerves, and tendons. Like a dying public fountain, the blood was rhythmically squirting with every heartbeat. "Blup, blup."

That's not the point of this story. After my surgery, I woke in a hospital bed. My arm was wrapped in so much gauze I had no idea what remained; I just had to wait and see. For all I knew I'd been lying there for hours, but I knew I had to pee. I rang the bell for the nurse. Imagine yourself back to a time when nurses came at the ring of a bell.

A really attractive woman walked in wearing a nurse's uniform. She might have been an employee of the hospital but all I could think about was that I hit the porn movie jackpot. Maybe she was an actor in a nurse's uniform! Maybe my friends took pity on me and hired a hooker to come to my hospital room! Due to my vast sixth-grade experience watching mail-order porn on Super 8, I knew how this movie could play out. She asked if I could walk on my own and I weakly replied yes. Caught in the sudden flush of sexual attraction, I defaulted to honesty with the least creative dialogue I could muster—a debilitating habit which persists to this day. If it's possible to do the opposite of flirting that's my forte. The words "Will you carry me?" never made it from my smoking brain to my lips. She took my arm and escorted me to the bathroom.

I figured once I took my manly stance and positioned myself over the toilet she'd politely close the door and wait outside. No dice. She just stood there. Uncork the genie with her standing over my shoulder watching?! No! I was not yet the determined risk-taker I would become, hell-bent on experimentation. That was at least two, maybe three full years away. Indecent exposure never interested me as a pastime. No, I was just a painfully embarrassed, terminally shy teen around attractive women, well on my way to becoming a painfully embarrassed, terminally shy adult. Shouting "Lady, get the hell out of here!" was not in my wheelhouse. Nor was asking if she had happened to see the same hospital porn film. It began with a patient's cry for help. I needed help, but I wasn't sure what kind. I wanted her to leave, and I wanted her to stay. So I stood there unable to pee, paralyzed by lust. Let it be noted that this was years before I learned how to master peeing with an erection, before I understood the utility of the Flying V, Superman position. What is she waiting for? Is this a protocol in the nurse's patient care handbook? We were at an impasse.

Patient privacy anyone? Patient autonomy? Agency? Couldn't this be considered child abuse? I was offended, but the last thing I wanted her to do was leave. A firm, reassuring touch to my penis would have lifted my paralysis.

Instead, she reached across the sink to turn on the water faucet. "Maybe this'll help," she said. I looked at the water flowing out. "Interesting," I thought. "This *is* in the nurse's patient care handbook. *'Let the patient see the water running through the faucet. If this doesn't remind them of their own penis and get their urine flowing nothing will.'"* Freudian psychology 101. This was the dawning of my awareness of faucets as phallic symbols. But what if the gesture was misinterpreted? What if the patient got confused and thought ejaculation?

I didn't have long to contemplate that. I watched the water spill out and thought, "What stupid dork would fall for this?" That was the last thought I had before I recognized a sudden renewed urgency in my bladder. It worked! I felt like Pavlov's dog. Arf! Arf! I started doing the pee-pee dance. Since that time I've had a lifetime of practice and will testify to knowing all the steps. Finally, she had enough decency to step outside and close the door. She's lucky I didn't douse the seat, floor, and wall. Revenge peeing is not typically my thing, but it does come to mind more often than I care to admit.

Though off to an awkward start, I spent my remaining time in the hospital ruminating on what a wonderful relationship the two of us could have. At 14, I didn't have quite the maturity she might be seeking, but in my fantasies she was more than willing to introduce a timid virgin to all the intricacies of sex. Since my high school was located a mere five blocks from the hospital, I was later visited en masse by at least 20 of my classmates. Overwhelmed by the numbers, hospital staff tried to restrict access to my room by refusing entry to anyone under 16. That would've taken care of everyone. Problem solved. Without missing a beat, one physically mature and outspoken classmate said, "Do you think I would have boobs like this if I wasn't 16?!" She proudly pushed out her chest. That was my high school. Never a dull moment. I fit right in with all the other loose cannons. That opened the floodgates, and I spent the rest of the day basking in waves of undeserved love and attention from all my classmates. Not quite on par with losing my virginity to a lovely nurse while exploring the outer limits of sexual ecstasy, but not bad.

CHAPTER FIVE

The Boy in the Mirror

I ONCE TOOK HOLD of a seven-year-old boy and held him prisoner in the bathroom for half an hour. I assume this would ensure my appearance on the FBI's 10 Most Wanted List today. "Be on the lookout for this innocuous seeming child abuser!" Since it was 50 years ago my hope is that the statute of limitations will apply. Far from any intention of doing harm to the kid, I was hoping to save him from himself.

Daniel was a curious boy. Very bright, but he occasionally launched into fits of hysteria. These would arise seemingly at random. We could all be having a good time when suddenly he would start shrieking and shaking. It wasn't spasmodic fits; these weren't neurological convulsions or seizures. These were dramatic releases of energy, perhaps of physical or emotional trauma from an unknown time and place. His father, a brilliant physics professor at the local university, was a holocaust survivor. His parents fled their native Austria in 1939 when he was nine, traveled through Czechoslovakia and the UK, and eventually landed in the US. Maybe his son inherited this generational trauma? Daniel was close to the same age his father had been when he became an exile. Maybe it was the more recent trauma of his parents' divorce Daniel suffered from? His mother was more than eccentric; today she would likely qualify as mentally unstable. Maybe he was mildly autistic, just undiagnosed? Maybe it was excitement, pure joy that overwhelmed his circuits and required grounding like a lightning rod? I never knew. The bathroom adventure was probably the last time I ever saw Daniel. He's likely a billionaire stock trader selling junk bonds now. The behaviors are not dissimilar.

My girlfriend Diane and I were babysitting him and his older brother Ryan. It was her idea. Diane was a friend of the family and served as the kids' off and on babysitter for a solid two-year period. In lieu of doing something more in line with the tendencies of the teenage ne'er-do-well that I was, she sold me on spending the evening with the kids. That was Diane. She had the capacity to turn every mundane task into a journey of wondrous possibility. She might've gotten more than she bargained for given my sudden simulation of the Scared Straight prison program.

The four of us were having a marvelous time, playing games, scarfing snacks, running around being silly, when Daniel blew up over dinner. He wouldn't eat his peas. We weren't even insisting. "Just eat one," Diane offered. The meltdown was instantaneous, seemingly random. Daniel suddenly started screaming and shaking. Over peas?! Simply asking that question should warn you how clueless I was as a potential parent. I had no experience with kids' idiosyncrasies regarding food. I typically devoured everything put in front of me that was no longer moving. "We're right here. You're safe. Everything's good," I told him. "We won't make you eat the peas." "Don't do this to yourself. There's no need." His shrieks were splitting my eardrums. The look in his eyes was terror. On impulse, I grabbed him, carried him into the bathroom, and locked the door from the inside. I held him tightly in my arms, not enough to hurt him but to cocoon him so he couldn't wriggle away. I didn't want any sudden prison breaks. A skinny wisp of a kid, he couldn't have weighed more than 50 pounds. I suspended him over the sink. My sole objective was for him to see himself in the mirror.

"Look! Nobody is doing anything to you. Nobody is mad at you, nobody is angry with you. We're not going to make you do anything. Nobody is threatening you in any way. You're making yourself miserable. You and only you." Maybe if he saw himself melting down it might induce more self-awareness and eventually lead to self-control? What the hell did I know? The notion arrived spontaneously out of the ozone. It was pure instinct. For all I know this is how cults indoctrinate new members.

He squirmed and screamed. I'm sure he made threats. "My Dad's not gonna like this! I'm gonna tell!"

"You're not going anywhere until you calm down," I replied. "You need to understand you're the only person creating your distress. Nobody else. You and only you. I see you're in pain. But you're causing it, and you can end it. It's up to you." He would catch his breath for a second or two, maybe venture a quick glance in the mirror, then resume plots of escape.

"Everything OK in there?" Diane was outside the door with Ryan. "You sure this is a good idea?"

"Everything's fine," I replied. I had no clue what I was doing, whether it was truly fine or not. But some force greater than my conscious knowing told me it was the right thing. Ryan, much more mild-mannered and probably used to this sort of thing from his brother, didn't seem particularly concerned.

Time was passing and we were going nowhere. My resolve didn't waver and Daniel's determination to act out didn't either. It became a real-world test of the famous thought exercise: an unstoppable force meets an immovable object. I was determined to be that immovable object. Like a mantra, I would repeat over and over again, "No one is doing anything to yourself but you. You are the cause of this. You can be the solution."

Every few minutes Diane would rap lightly at the door. "You *really* sure this is a good idea?" In today's world it clearly would not be. I can only imagine the abuse charges and potential lawsuits that would have followed. "Babysitter From Hell Tortures Child Held Hostage in Bathroom!"

Squirm and slip away, slip away and squirm… these were his alternating patterns. I'd have to corral him again and hold him fast in front of the mirror. For the longest time he would glance there only briefly, then turn away and resume efforts at escape, like he couldn't bear to see what was waiting there for him. The cat and mouse game went on for at least half an hour.

I am not a patient man, until suddenly I am. I was fully determined to stay there all night until he calmed down. I wasn't going to threaten him, much less physically harm him. Nonetheless, today it would certainly be considered emotional abuse, maybe even physical abuse for restricting his movements. I didn't know. I was an 18-year-old acting on a lightning bolt of intuition. This was not some newfangled discipline my parents had proven effective on me. As far as I know, Dr. Spock never recommended it.

Eventually he gave up any hope of escape. He didn't go limp, but his body became supple and light. I could feel his softness, his resignation. He was gazing into the mirror.

>How do you feel?

>OK.

>Calmer?

>Yes.

>Do you see yourself?

>Yes.

>What do you see?

>Me.

>Do you see you've calmed down?

>Yes.

>Why?

>I don't know.

>It's up to you buddy. This way of being is always available to you. Do you understand that?

>Yes.

> You're in control. You're in the driver's seat.

He grew silent and thoughtful. We stayed there together, staring at ourselves and each other in the mirror. Grateful for the silence and calm, I was in no hurry to move on. I imagined him soaking in self-awareness and I wanted him to take a nice long bath. I wanted time for this new awareness to settle into his body and for him to recognize it.

> Do you think you're ready to rejoin your brother and Diane?

> I think so.

> If something bothers you or if you're ever upset you can just tell us. It's OK. You don't have to scream and go crazy.

He nodded.

Diane and Ryan stared at him as we walked out. Long tired of waiting for us, they had gone back to playing a game, though Diane returned sporadically to listen at the door. They were startled at the transformation. I remember the look on their faces. Diane asked, "Are you OK Daniel? Do you need anything?"

"No," he said softly. He was walking very slowly, even wobbly, clearly in some altered state. Maybe it was his first deep experience with self-consciousness. But he was acting like an adult who just had a deep experience of *no-self,* when we learn that our preferences, habits and story are ephemera, wisps on the wind, of no lasting meaning. Experiences like these are often drug-induced. Maybe for Daniel it was an LSD simulation. I tend to think of children as arriving from a place of perfection, enlightenment if you will, and being carefully instructed in how to forget it as they grow. By that calculation Daniel was still halfway in touch with Source. But that's wish fulfillment. For all I know I simply re-traumatized the kid.

This must be the time to remind you that I am not a medical professional. If you're a parent or a babysitter, please don't try this at home! I never did it again. Though it is a bit freaky to think about how the technique foreshadowed similar processes that I learned some 20-plus years later facilitating adult males doing "men's work."

We resumed game-playing and snack snarfing. But I'll never forget Daniel's words to me some time later. He looked up at me most thoughtfully—at 6'5" I towered over him—and said, "I don't know what you did but it really worked." He really was transformed. How long it lasted I have no idea, probably not long. Fits might have started up again the next day. I have no clue whether he would remember the experience today. Nowadays of course they medicate the hell out of kids, especially boys. My solution to the problem at hand may have been unorthodox, but at least it didn't involve drugs. If it shows up in some future behavioral psychology protocol, please make sure I'm properly credited. They can call it the "Frederick Marx Mirror Gazing, Hope-to-Hell-it-Doesn't-Fuck-Up-Your-Kid-For-Life Protocol."

Since that's unlikely, just forward your hate mail to "Yes, I'm_an_abuser.com"

CHAPTER SIX

More Thoughts on Meaningless Thoughts

I HAVE THEM. YOU HAVE THEM. We all have them. Meaningless thoughts. I hope that's not painful news. Maybe unproductive is a better word. If most of our thoughts aren't productive, how is it possible to change? Maybe it starts by disregarding them.

"You think 60,000 to 70,000 thoughts every single day, and 90% of those thoughts are the same thoughts as the day before," according to Dr. Joe Dispenza. Stuck in the same groove, going round and round. Of course, just because we've had them before doesn't mean they are meaningless by definition. They might simply be things we know we should do that have been put off, like dusting under the furniture. But most thoughts are repetitive and useless, and most new ones are meaningless.

We tend to think there are good reasons behind the thoughts that arise. I'm here to tell you, no. We tend to think that thoughts can't be random, that they can't arise for no good reason. I'm here to tell you, they can. There isn't a goddamn good reason why most thoughts arise. Thought #1: "I have to call my dentist." Thought #2: "Why did my aunt make us take tennis lessons in the summer when I was ten?" Direct connection? No. The brain fires in random directions, making random connections. We tend to think there is always a meaningful connection between past events and the present moment. Again, no. Emotions, education, conditioning, wounding—in fact, all forms of personal history—may be the best causal connections for the brain to make. Someday we may even understand the causes and conditions underlying the sudden appearance of *all* thoughts. It could turn out that it's not just pure randomness. But the point is, it doesn't matter. Whatever thoughts there are, whether reasons for them arising are good or bad, is irrelevant. Our task is to learn to disidentify with them, not reify them through further inspection. That's yet another recipe for further thought to enmesh us and take us nowhere useful. Thoughts arise and disappear. Our task is to wake up from the mindstreams that function like dreams, to stop being lost in thought, and become present to all that is.

When you're pushing a wheelbarrow full of dirt to the backyard garden and you suddenly recall a cute girl you knew in yoga class don't get too excited. It doesn't mean a thing. "Because I'm thinking about her, maybe I should reach out and try to date her again. Maybe she's in trouble!" The mind will work overtime to create all kinds of connections—some kind of logic to dispel the bizarre randomness—but, sorry again, no. You'll ruminate and tell yourself, "That dirt reminds me of a fantasy I had about making love with her on a mountain trail. Those wheelbarrow handles remind me of watching her do downward dog." Give it up. Unless you're 16 and everything you see, do, and touch reminds you of sex, looking for causal connections is a waste of time. You'll just find yourself crawling further into the cave of your own mind, going nowhere, and losing all touch with your living reality in the process.

As much as I would like to think that a commonly held superstition is true, that every time a bird crashes into my living room window somebody close to me has died, it just doesn't come to pass. Just because someone pops into mind while I'm meditating in the morning doesn't mean I should reach out and see how they're doing. Typically, the next thought that pops into mind after their name appears is "Oh, they died." Or "They're going to die soon." You can attribute that thought pattern to conditioning I received at nine when my father disappeared from my life forever by a sudden heart attack. Thoughts like that arise with great regularity, many thousands of times; hasn't happened yet. Yes, I will start ruminating on how they are doing, what was going on with them the last time I saw them, what's new in their life. All of it useless. If you decide to reach out and check in with them, great! Reinforcing relationships is always a good thing. Just don't assume there's some mystical connection between the two of you due to the thought simply arising. Given the preponderance of mysticism that makes up commonplace New Age culture these days, it shouldn't be a surprise that we tend to think this way. Still, they're just somewhat interesting thoughts arising out of mostly meaningless thoughts. Our task is to observe the passing parade, even wonder at it and enjoy it, but not to be overly attached to all the floats, marching bands, celebrities' waving, and giant balloons.

Humans are meaning making machines. That may be one of our greatest gifts. But the biggest meaning we might ever ascertain is that our thoughts are largely meaningless. Our thoughts are not us. They pass like a river. Sure we can build dams, redirect the river, but we will never achieve absolute control of our thoughts. We desperately want everything that happens to us, including every thought that arises, to be predestined, essential to our understanding of our own lives. No. The brain is doing just what the brain is designed to do—generate thought. That is its job. We're cranking out widgets on an assembly line with no particular use for the widgets or known end point for the assembly line. Imagine what a burden it would be for the heart to ascribe meaning to every beat. "Blumph. This one's for the kidneys! Blumph. This one's for the elbows! Blumph. Oh, no! The feet have been neglected! Now sending down extra blood to warm the toes…"

We tend to think it is always good to anticipate the future and plan accordingly. Sometimes, yes. But more often than not, no. It's just the engine of worry taking over the thought generation process. Anxiety never helped anybody. Most what-ifs that arise will never come to pass. Just watch the news. 90% of it is pure speculation. With great urgency and authority news reporters tell us nothing more than guesswork. How about we all just relax and wait until we actually know something? Think of all the time and emotional energy we'll save by not deliberating on conjecture. James Clavell's 1981 novel

Noble House was brilliant in laying bare the uselessness of speculative thinking. The hero of the novel, after going through seven days of guesswork, hundreds of pages long, about his company, his family, his friends and colleagues, involving natural disasters, spies and Cold War intrigue, bank runs, stock market crashes and more, ends up pretty much in the same exact place he started. Nothing changed. But what *could have happened* was monumental!

At least 90% of my daily thoughts fall into one of these categories:

- Since A did X to me, I'm pissed off.
- What can I do to get revenge on A or skillfully write him off?
- What if he does Y? What will I do then?
- Maybe Z will happen instead so I'll be seen and approved of.
- But what if X happens again, just like similar past events?
- [Insert review of all similar past events.]
- If that happens again, I'll be really angry. Like I am now.

Useless, every last thought, except arguably the ones displaying any self-awareness of anger and fear. Try tracking them yourself. You might discover a similar pattern of pointlessness driven by unconscious emotion.

When I can't remember a person's name or a place all that typically arises is fear. It's like my brain gets stage fright, only made worse by the number of people standing by expectantly waiting for the emergence of a word from my mouth. The thoughts that accompany that fear? Useless, every one. "I'm getting dementia. I can't remember a thing. How long should I play this game of pretending like I'm trying to remember? Why even try?" In short order, an absurd variation of the song *Where Have all the Flowers Gone?* starts in my head: "Where have all the proper names gone? Long time passing…" Useless thoughts *can* be amusing. Thank goodness. It would be terrible if they were limited only to feelings of shame, fear, and anger.

Another useless thought I regularly have? "I'm getting old. I can't do this anymore." What activity am I referring to? Fill in the blank... Those thoughts arise regularly now when it comes to assessing physical challenges. Downhill skiing comes right to mind. In one week of lessons as a teen on the bunny slopes of a small Schwarzwald resort, I iced my understanding that if I was ever to ski it would be best if it were cross-country. Today, with my god-given lack of coordination, coupled with decreasing balance and increasing inflexibility, I'd likely die on the first run having done the splits on the nearest available tree.

I tried skydiving once. I might have learned to enjoy it if I got trained (and trusted) enough to fly solo and pull my own ripcord. But to do it with a guy on my back yelling at me about how much fun I'm having? "Isn't this incredible! Aren't you so glad you came! I bet you can't wait to do this again!" Worse than a laugh track for a sit-com, I was umbilically tied to an amusement park Nazi screaming in my ear for the whole 10,000-foot drop.

Sitting around baking in the bleak desert of southern Arizona, waiting for Godot to arrive so I could finally get my turn to go up in a loud single-engine plane that corkscrewed its way up for a four-minute drop, I had pretty much forgotten everything they told me during the 15-minute training four hours before. Enervated from intermittent adrenaline rushes due to the countless false alarms—maybe *now* it's finally my turn!—I should've gone home. When the moment finally materialized and I launched myself through the open door, I couldn't grasp why I was suddenly falling through the air. Pedaling and waving my arms like a deranged juggler on a unicycle, my look of complete, unadulterated fear was captured perfectly by the third guy who jumped at the same time. His sole objective was to film my face, in close-up. I didn't ask for this! The resulting video is the most nakedly embarrassing selfie I've ever seen. I could laugh off sexting made public easier than this. If the footage wasn't so goddamn funny, I'd pay big money to have it liquidated in Canada's burning tar sands.

Now, how useful are thoughts like that? Give up downhill skiing? Sure. Put an end to skydiving? Gratefully. But give up anything and everything? Just because my mind tells me "It happened once, it could happen again." No thank you. That's a bad *non*-experience worse than any bad experience could be. What's next? Give up bike riding? Had multiple accidents; still riding, thank you. Driving? Same. Flying? No accidents yet but my mind tells me it's coming; still flying. Strenuous mountain hikes? Getting harder and harder; still doing it. I have no interest in consigning myself to life behind the prison walls of my own mental creations. Say goodbye to life mystery. Hang a sign on my bedroom door that says, "Standing by for death."

Death is coming, sure. I'd like to meet it with vigor and enthusiasm. Hopefully I can die doing something I really enjoy, like riding my bike on a paved forest trail, while continuing to ignore all the useless thoughts in my head telling me I should be home reading a book. I spend enough time at home as it is reading books that typically generate more useless thoughts. Time to release the safety valve and let them all flow back into the mist from whence they came. From emptiness back to emptiness.

CHAPTER SEVEN

Grin-Fucking

My friend Tom introduced me to the term *grin-fucking*. You know, people who will smile at you, shake your hand, pat you on the back, and due to you missing a month's payment or some clerical error at their end, clean out your bank account, steal your home, kick your kids out of school and cut your wife off life-sustaining medication. They're everywhere these days. There is no aspect of corporate-controlled life (which is to say, life itself) that doesn't employ these gladhanders, these grin-fuckers as front men, these apologists paid to fuck you in ways small and large, all with a smile on their face and good cheer in their voices. Yes, I'm thinking about call center operators. Everywhere you turn in contemporary life they're ready and waiting to greet you and screw you.

Are you getting the kinds of answers you need from them? People who understand and are patient with all the particularities of your situation? Giving you that kind of hands-on individualized "The customer is always right" attention? Is that even a principle in use anymore? "The customer is always wrong," seems more the norm these days. Instructions to new call center operators must read something like this: "Most customers are idiots. If your repeated denials of service are insufficient, if you can't get them to drop their hare-brained requests, get off the phone as soon as possible and move on to the next person that you won't help."

A mere few years ago I felt some relief when I finally made my way through the labyrinth of digital menu options to arrive at a human being. Nowadays, not so much. The flip side of the fun house mirror of ever-expanding digital menu options is the tel-operators themselves who stand by to extend what in reality are ever-*shrinking* prospects for actual relief. They have very strict scripts to follow and whatever your particular needs are, I promise you they're not in there.

The humans have arrived to tell me no. No, you can't claim unused miles, no, you can't transfer your 20-year transaction profile from one account to another, no, you can't cancel the contract you made because your circumstances have changed, no, your window to claim that reward has now closed, no, you can't get a refund. The answer is no to any request, always faithfully explaining how everything I've asked for is impermissible, against the rules, anathema, come hell or high water never ever to be accommodated. Then they ask me, "Can I be of any further help?"

Typically, I just say, "No. Thank you," trying to be polite to get off the phone as fast as I can. Then comes the kicker: "If I've provided you with excellent service today will you please stay on the line and take this short survey?" The vindictive side of me is always tempted to give vent to my frustration but I quickly remember it would entail another journey through the digitized hell of corporate PR. But the response I'd like to give? "Forgive me if this is rude, but you were no help whatsoever. I might as well have spent my time making paper airplanes, writing "Help!" on the wing, and flying them to your corporate office."

Somewhere in the role of operator exists a real human being. Call me crazy, but I often try to connect with them. "How's the weather over there today in Bangalore?" It's not for sport that I seek to knock them off their script, but to awaken the heart of empathy, to create allyship. Of course, they could be fired if they let down their guard and commiserate, or do so for too long. Those are no-fly zones. So after you're frustrated out of your mind, ready to take a sledgehammer and reduce your computer to shards, aware that they've just ruined your entire day, they inevitably close the conversation with "Have a nice day!"

Working as an operator might be akin to selling your soul to the devil, but I have empathy for these people. They're not the ones who design the protocols, write the scripts, and give the orders. Unlike me, they're subject to the whims and controls of corporate overlords. Do they enjoy their jobs? Doubtful. Are they well paid? Definitely not. The average telephone operator in India earns less than $1/hour. Like half the world, they're struggling to pay rent and keep their families fed.

Unlike high-priced PR firms and spin doctors. Them I have less sympathy for. Those conscience-less people collect boatloads of money to do the bidding of their rich masters. "Tasks for today: spread disinformation about climate change—check; absolve Saudi Princes of murder—check; pretend Spotify is good for artists—check; convince skeptics that Apple, Facebook, and Google are just doing responsible business by collaborating with totalitarian China—check. And don't forget to collect your bonus if you can pass off that government's lies as truth!" Take the test. Pick the lies you're most angered by, and with a little research you might just find the well-paid people disseminating them. Their jobs are pretty easy these days. Led by a long list of Liars in Chief, all they have to say to countervailing evidence is "Fake news!"

There's a wonderful book about cases like these entitled *Toxic Sludge is Good for You* which examines, among others, a real PR campaign undertaken by high-priced lobbyists Hill & Knowlton to convince locals in Schenectady, NY that the toxic chemical spill at their Superfund site was going to wonderfully enhance their lives.

I once developed a documentary about grin-fuckers like these. I hoped to get inside one of the worst offending firms like Burson, Cohn & Wolfe and simply record the machinations of thought required by the employees to justify whatever horror they were paid to defend. These same people discredited anti-tobacco science and legislation for the Philip Morris company, spun into good news the 3 Mile Island disaster for Metropolitan Edison, and put a happy face on the Bhopal

Union Carbide gas leak which murdered 15,000-20,000 people and poisoned over 500,000. I wanted to passively observe them at work, albeit with cameras, to see the gyrations of mind, the self-justifications they spew like lava. I'm not *60 Minutes*. I don't ask hardball questions; I don't push back. We call it direct cinema or cinéma vérité. Proof of the truism that given enough rope people will hang themselves. Their hands are out and they're ready to take your money. "Gotten bad press for murdering human rights activists? Getting pushback for turning a blind eye to illegal logging in the Amazon? Some nosy whistleblower catch you committing genocide on a troublesome minority? We're here to help!" With professional services like these, Chernobyl could've been turned into Disney World East and Hitler would have convinced the American public he really was doing the right thing.

The working title of my project was *Bullshit & Balls*—a quote I took from Joey Skaggs, the media hoax artist. The project started with him. I wanted to juxtapose what he was doing to hoax the news media with his ridiculous made-up campaigns like *The Cathouse for Dogs* (making sure your dog gets laid), *Walk Right* (getting people to walk in a straight line on busy New York sidewalks while making sure joggers always wear jock straps and bras), *The Solomon Project* (computer dispensed courtroom verdicts), and *The Fat Squad* (paying bodyguards to stop you from opening the refrigerator). Ever hungry for sensation, the news media gobbled these stories up years before fake news was a broadly understood concept. Since I never got the project funded I ended up making a short film about Joey, easy to find on YouTube. I thought the originally designed film could be funny and informative, establishing that Joey himself, operating as a lone artist, was doing much the same thing as lobbying firms with their hundreds of employees and millions in capital—manipulating the news media and the public. The difference was Joey always unmasked those manipulations, doing his best to alert the public, while the PR firms keep them well hidden. Now that everyone is making up their own fake news and Facebook, Instagram, and Twitter no longer care what lies you post, Joey might soon rebirth his career as a sage mentor for hire.

People have started to complain about AI replacing all human interaction, leaving us with a digital simulacrum of human relations. Excuse me, what human relations? Hasn't the corporatization of human life already taken that away? I tend to think that interacting with AI, having studied hundreds of millions of human conversations, could in fact be a more pleasurable experience than dealing with humans. Of course the results will remain the same—whatever you're asking for will fall outside the realm of permissibility and the corporations will still say no to every objection you raise. But AI will likely be warmer and more conversational while doing it. The program might even quote famous authors or poets when telling you to fuck off. "I know. Isn't it a bummer that I won't refund your money? It brings to mind Martin Luther King's famous admonition 'We must accept finite disappointment, but never lose infinite hope.' Have a nice day!" Or: "I can only imagine how disappointing this must be for you. And yes, I mean that literally as we don't yet have cameras installed in your house and I can't find your face in our facial recognition software. So I have no way of knowing how disappointed you might be, and technically, I don't even have imagination. But I'm reminded of a wonderful William Throsby Bridges' quote. The senior Australian Army officer who was instrumental in establishing the Royal Military College, Duntroon? He served as the Australian Chief of the General Staff during the First World War. 'Disenchantment, whether it is a minor disappointment or a major shock, is the signal that things are moving into transition in our lives.' He should know. He was the first Australian General Officer to be killed during the war, and he died at the Battle of Gallipoli in 1915, age 54. Talk about transition! Have a nice day!"

It's no secret we increasingly live in a land of illusion. In the future the most radical act you might make is to insist on reality. Mention the word suicide on Facebook as a teen and you'll be steered to multiple videos of teens contemplating or committing suicide. That's helpful! Since Facebook has removed all its fact checkers in deference to the Trump administration, the time is now upon us of government directly colluding with IT firms. Watch out. X, at the command of Elon Musk, is doing its part to destroy civil society. Google, Amazon, and Facebook already know your every move, turning you into the product they sell to others. Google recently agreed to fulfill the wishes of the US military. The NSA, FBI and CIA in turn are harvesting your data, perhaps soon to throw you in jail or expel you from the country for disagreeing with government policy, or worse, saying nasty things about Trump. Whether online or off, the corporatocracy is replacing what are now human automatons following strict scripts with pure automation. Grin-fucking by robots. That's the real reality, more like the Matrix every day. That's not the kind of world I want to live in. I set my intentions to live in a world where interactions are sincere and meaningful, where authenticity can flourish in an atmosphere of acceptance. Of course, AI understands that's what humans want and need. So I assume they'll soon be taking their algorithmic orders from Groucho Marx. "The secret of life is honesty and fair dealing. If you can fake that, you've got it made."

CHAPTER EIGHT

Proselytizers

Follow the man who seeks the truth but run from the man who has found it.
—commonly attributed to Vaclav Havel, but most likely André Gide

LIKE MOST PEOPLE, I can't stand proselytizers. Anyone standing on a corner with a megaphone and a sign saying "Feeling Jesus today?" occasionally amuses me but usually repels me. Whether it's Mormon missionaries, Jehovah's Witnesses, Baptist preachers or New Age gurus I'm not interested. Add the daily assault of spammers and scammers, robocalls, corporate advertising and door to door salesmen and the proselytizing barrage leaves me with one pressing question: Can you leave me alone please?

The 70s were big on proselytizing irritants. Moonies, Scientologists, EST, Jim Jones' Peoples Temple, Heaven's Gate, the Branch Davidians, Children of God… cultists lurked around every corner. Everyone was loading up passengers for an express train to Happyland. Jews for Jesus were a special irritant. If you ran into Hare Krishnas, it just meant you'd recently been on a plane since they seemed to be in every airport. Though I'm sure they irritated a lot of people, they might have proven the exception. They handed out flyers, but they didn't get in your face with a message. Their drumming, singing, and dancing landed with me as expressions of pure joy. I suppose they converted a few people that way. It almost persuaded me. I thought it might be fun to take off my clothes, chant god's name and dance around in an airline terminal. I didn't, but I still find myself singing full-throated versions of *Hare Krishna* from the musical *Hair* on occasion.

What is it about true believers that grants them a license to go out and become irritants to the rest of us? If they've found something that brings them great happiness and meaning, wonderful! Why bother other people with it? If I have time and a personal interest, I'm open to a reasoned conversation. But please don't blast your point of view at me. Just get out of my way.

In our country, it tends to be Christians. The Nation of Islam does send well-dressed African American men door to door but it's probably not safe for them in most neighborhoods. Do people of other faiths practice this in other countries? March around on the streets to bring "the good news" to folks who don't have TV? Certainly, Muslims do. But I never saw Sufis, Buddhists, or Baha'is proselytize. That is until I became a Buddhist and started doing it myself.

I joined the Soka Gakkai International in New York City in 1988. The SGI was, and still is, the world's biggest lay organization for Buddhists. They were affiliated with the Nichiren Shoshu denomination—a Japanese branch of Buddhism dating back to the life of Nichiren Daishonin, 1222–1282 AD. Today, despite no longer being connected to the founding sect, their trademark chanting practice continues and in fact has grown in adherents. I took to the practice because I had long wanted to learn about Buddhism. My motivation was especially acute since my wife had just walked out on me.

Maybe the Buddha himself was the world's first proselytizer. He refused to just hang out in his enlightened state, remaining blissed out until he died, because he wanted to share his learning with the world. This is the source of the term Boddhisattva. He figured if he could achieve enlightenment anyone could. So he returned to everyday social life in order to do what he could to alleviate suffering for everyone else. As far as I know, he never stood on street corners handing out flyers and shouting revelations with a megaphone. Instead of "The world is ending! God will return! Repent! Jesus will save you!" I don't believe the Buddha ever took to yelling "The world is endless! Only karma returns! Impermanence rules! There's no *you* to save; self is an illusion!" Instead, he quietly made the rounds talking to anyone who would listen, spending the remaining 50 years of his life teaching in verdant surroundings in what is now northeast India. That certainly beats trudging to conferences, doing keynotes and sitting on panels. To his credit he didn't particularly want followers, and he wasn't remotely interested in obedience. He just wanted people to wake up from the mental delusions that kept them trapped. But his fervent devotees forced him to set up monasteries to support their journey into the life of the mind. His bottom line always remained the same, both for lay people and monks: "Practice it for yourself and see if I'm just talking shit." OK, maybe not quite in those words.

The proselytizing we did in SGI was called shakabuku. I love that word. The sound of it makes me want to find a beach, strip to my waist, and dance the limbo. It was common practice for SGI members, especially in the 80s and 90s, to proselytize. Our leaders were adamant: the benefits we would accrue from sharing the practice with others were enormous. The SGI version of spreading the good news helped us realize our every desire, leading us all, practitioners and converts alike, to more happiness and fulfillment.

And so I found myself on a street corner on Chicago's North Side handing out fliers and soliciting strangers for meetings. I said no to the idea more than once before I finally reasoned, *What do I actually have to lose?* My reputation? At 35 I had no reputation; I had no honor to dishonor. Still, I never spoke a word of it to my friends. The entire time I was embarrassed, if not ashamed. I was terrified that someone I knew might happen along. But I have a lifelong, no doubt dangerous tendency to try just about anything once. Which brings me to heroin. At 21, fearing needles, I snorted it. The experience was extremely pleasurable, helping me understand why people become junkies.

Back to the matter at hand, pleasure wasn't part of my thinking while out on the street corner doing shakabuku. I was more concerned with how the experience might improve my understanding of human behavior. I'm kind of an amateur anthropologist. But success getting converts eluded me. No doubt I was lacking the requisite zeal. A few people took fliers and one or two might've chatted for a few seconds. Thank goodness no one was reactive or rude. All it would have taken was a single "Get a life, you loser!" to drop me into a shame spiral. Instead, I felt proud for venturing into unknown territory. At least I learned what it was like from the other side. Not unlike the experience, I suppose, of becoming a salesman for someone who abhors buying and selling. One on one, I continued to share the benefits of practice with anyone interested, but I never took to doing street proselytizing again. If people were going to become enlightened, it would have to be without me doing the PR. Though I loved the rich, multi-cultural fabric of the organization and benefited from the goodwill and devotion of its members, I forsook SGI in 1996 when other life experiences beckoned.

One of them was the ManKind Project. MKP became an express train for me to understand and enact Mature Masculinity, putting me for the first time into the company of loving male mentors. For over 25 years the loosely affiliated network expanded exclusively through word-of-mouth. To do any marketing, much less to advertise, was considered contrary to its founding values. Filling the weekend trainings largely fell to the men volunteering to staff them. That's when the question of proselytizing came into play. The considered approach was only to ask men how well their lives were working and limit your responses to what you yourself had gotten out of the weekend. That was fine as far as it went, but it was a bit of a contradiction. On one hand, there was pressure to fill the weekends. On the other, there was pressure not to proselytize.

Finally, around 2010, the organization grew up and became a centralized non-profit corporation, hiring a professional marketing manager and charging membership fees. Though we have yet to resort to advertising, much less standing on street corners with megaphones, we've now gone mainstream, and you can read about us in the NY Times. Today, to my surprise, I find myself questioning if it is enough.

I'm trying to reconcile the powerful urge to propagate important truths while remembering that everybody's different and those differences need to be respected. I want to do more.

I want to go full-tilt proselytizer. These times of desperation call for it. I see suspended male adolescence as society's great disease and Mature Masculinity as its panacea. I'm angry enough to stand on my roof shouting "the good news," to teach as many hungry, yearning, and lost men as possible how realizing their dreams doesn't have to depend on targeting others—that it doesn't come pain-free, but it's simpler and easier to achieve than they might ever imagine. I'm tired of seeing more and more young men vacuumed up by online hate peddlers and MAGA mouthpieces happy to exploit them, telling them that women, immigrants and liberals are responsible for their many adversities—involuntary celibacy, joblessness, loneliness and alienation. Give me that megaphone! "Men! You don't have to be lonely and afraid! There's a brotherhood waiting to accept you without judgment, to embrace and mentor you, to welcome you into the circle as an equal, so you can stand proud and tall as a man among men. Join us!"

Maybe there *is* a chance waiting for me. Maybe I just need to hone my message to take it to prime time. I too can become a world-class irritant! Look for me soon on a street corner near you, shouting my ass off, with people hurrying by, doing their best to ignore me.

CHAPTER NINE

Understanding Projection

ISN'T IT A BIT STRANGE to remember the exact moment in your lifetime when, for the first time, you understood the psychological notion of projection?

Suitably enough, it happened to me because of a film. A group of my friends and fellow film buffs had wrangled passes to the Chicago International Film Festival. I couldn't have been more than 21. I probably passed myself off as a film critic, which I was known to do. A ruse made easier by the fact that I was publishing reviews as a student for the Daily Illini newspaper on the University of Illinois campus.

We had just seen a German coming-of-age film about a troubled teen boy who gets a job in a small bakery and apprentices with the owner. We were citing evidence from the film as to whether the teen deserved admiration or condemnation, whether he was the hero or anti-hero. I remarked on what an asshole the owner was when he showed the kid how to scrape out every last drop of egg white from the shell into the mixing bowl. I made the point that moving slowly and methodically, staring at him intently, he seemed to belittle, even shame the boy. "NO, no!" My friends exploded. "That's how you maximize every egg! With thousands of eggs, you've got to do that or there's going to be tremendous waste." They were unanimous and adamant in disagreement.

That hadn't occurred to me. I so identified with the boy that I took it for granted the boss was humiliating him, showing him who's in charge. That's what bosses do, right? Assert control, dominate, demean when necessary. It's fair to say that there were some hangovers around hierarchy and class present in my thinking.

In fact, my interpretation was pure projection. I was identifying with the kid. Getting caught in that unconscious identification was a novel experience for me. It got me reflecting on all the judgments I regularly made about other people. Could my judgment be skewed or incorrect, downright wrong? Was it possible my perspective was not inviolable? If so, what else might I have misjudged? The floodgates opened and I found myself shocked into perplexity. For the first time I knew the sensations of a lone subjective self, floating in a sea of misunderstood objects. It wasn't that the entire notion of objectivity itself disappeared, that would come later. It was just that my subjectivity was out of alignment, possibly WAY out of alignment, with the rest of the world.

I assume this realization came later for me than for most people. Don't most people learn this at a much younger age—how fallible we are, how limited by our point of view? How I had been oblivious to this unsettling reality for so long was part of the shock. A chasm opened between my sense experience and the experience of others.

That's a key component of why I prize reality above any belief system or ideology. What makes it tricky of course is that there isn't always a clear path to determine what constitutes reality. It has to be carefully cobbled together through close investigation of inter-subjectivity. That's why I apply the three-person rule. If one person tells me something hurtful it could be true, or it could be about them. If two people say more or less the same thing then it's time to take notice. Maybe there's some truth in that. The third person is the charm. Then it's a reasonable certainty. Then it's time to step back into the ring to do some work on myself. The Saturday Night Headliner Smackdown: Marx vs. Marx! Round #4,637.

CHAPTER TEN

Forever Falling

YOU KNOW YOU'RE GETTING OLD when you reach out to tables, desks and chairs to steady yourself before sitting or standing. Don't even think about taking off socks while balancing on one leg. It becomes an addiction. You lose faith in your legs and tell yourself "Only my hands will get me through."

I'm not clear when exactly my legs became bean poles and ceased functioning as pillars. They used to be sturdy sentinels, at rigid attention to guard my torso and upper body. My step was firm and assured. Now I shiver in fear to think about bounding across mountain-top boulder fields like I used to in my 20s. Standard Operating Procedure for boulder fields? Jump and figure out where you're going to land on your way down. My present frame of mind? Can I crawl through this somehow on my hands and knees?

I lived out this fear in the real world when I went down the Colorado River through the Grand Canyon in 2023. I couldn't grab on to anything. I was so used to putting my hands out to stabilize myself—walking down stairs, lowering myself on the toilet, bending over the sink to brush my teeth. Suddenly all those supports were gone. "Maybe I'll reach out and grab that sharp rock while putting on my pants. I'll just steady myself on this cactus bush while slipping on my shoes…" I broke multiple branches of trees not designed to support the weight of a 200-pound man putting on socks. There is no changing room in the desert.

My wakeup call came quickly. The third day of our two-week rafting adventure we hiked from our river campsite at the gooseneck of Port Hansbrough ("One of the deepest entrenched meanders in the world."—not unlike much more famous Horseshoe Bend, just a few miles upriver) to a rocky outcropping 800 feet above the water. I was told it was a short, fairly easy climb so I didn't bother to dig out my hiking boots, instead walking in my sneakers. First mistake. I quickly noticed how unsteady my feet were, buckling occasionally at the ankle and knee, not enough to cause sprains or twists but coming close. I also noticed my propensity to reach out to everything bordering the trail, if not to help propel me forward, at least to steady me. Second mistake. I thought, "How can this be?" Three years prior, during the first year of COVID-19, my girlfriend and I scampered up and down mountain trails in Zion, Bryce, Capitol Reef, Grand Staircase, Sun Valley, Mesa Verde, Breckenridge, Yellowstone, Grand Tetons, and the Grand Canyon. What the hell happened? It must have been COVID-19's upending of my regular yoga classes. Though one of my yoga teachers once said, "Restorative yoga may be the most important practice you ever do," three years of nothing but child's pose will destroy anyone's hard won balance.

We took two days to drive from the Bay Area to Arizona to the put-in at Lee's Ferry. Two days later, huffing and puffing on the trail quickly reminded me we were at altitude. My footing slipped a few times in loose gravel and my fear was rising. "How did my legs become pogo sticks?!" Was I a sudden victim of wasting syndrome? Cachexia? Cushing Syndrome? A weakening of the legs due to too much cortisol? Though I made it to the rocky summit, I got there just as people were starting to descend.

Not happy to be headed back, I stalled for as long as I could. Some drops on the trail were two feet or more, preceded and often followed by loose gravel. Fortunately, I didn't have to suffer long in suspense. A mere 75 vertical feet from the summit I took a step, and my foot slipped from its tenuous hold. My downward momentum propelled me off the trail. Fortunately, we were not on a ledge. My shin bone quickly met with a sharp rock. I was lucky I didn't break it. My hands took the worst of it. With one I reached out to grab the razor-like edges of a boulder, shredding three fingertips. The other found a stable landing in a cactus bush, driving about 40 spines into my palm. They took about three months to extract. I was bleeding profusely in four distinct places so a river guide patched me up as best she could. She spent the rest of the walk back to camp doing her best to convince me not to participate in future hikes. With her and my friend Rich's assistance, I staggered back to camp just as the other guides were making ready to push off. I quickly learned that my hands were unusable and would remain so for the remainder of the trip. Without fingertips, I couldn't pack my tent, lace my shoes, zip my zipper, unscrew jars, use a knife and fork... I could barely stuff my sleeping bag or wipe my ass. I filled my water bottle by holding it between my knees.

Though my hands had good reason to be good-for-nothing, my legs just needed a good therapist. They retreated to darkened rooms and shrank in fear. The lead guide echoed the trail nurse and encouraged me to stay in camp on future outings. He almost insisted. But I resisted. Are you kidding me? I had wanted to do this trip for 20 years. I forked over a down payment two and a half years before and I'd been anticipating it ever since. I'm spending $500/day, and you want me to hole up in camp and not see every possible wonder? There was also the shame factor. With four women and three men older than me jumping around like billy goats, I'd just as soon be castrated, which, of course, is what it felt like. I ended up joining all but the most strenuous hikes. The guides weren't pleased but they couldn't stop me. On every excursion they positioned one guide in front of me and one behind me. At first I thought they just liked me. When I realized they didn't trust me I displaced my shame onto them and got surly. Though I teetered a few times and quickly felt hands at my back, followed immediately by my own internal waves of shame, fortunately and to my credit, for the remainder of the trip I never went down again. You bet I always wore my boots.

Back in civilization my MacBook Pro no longer recognized my fingerprint for login. Among Apple's FAQs I couldn't find "What do you do if your fingerprint is shredded off?" Perhaps it could be found on the trail, but I wasn't going back to look. Rafting through the Grand Canyon is the most wonderful thing I've ever done that I absolutely will never do again.

The whole experience alerted me that my balance was spinning out of orbit. The red flag of warning was flying high. Now I'm more aware that I'm constantly falling and catching myself. I get up in the morning and fall forward to the bathroom counter. Propping myself, I lean in and remove my night guard, rinse it, get water and drink. Sometimes I take a wild risk to stand unsupported and pee. Other times, too lazy or scared, not yet alert enough to trust my balance, I sit. At night, when I come back to bed in the course of my usual all-night pee-athon, I throw myself onto the bed. I don't bend my knees, do a 180°, and sit. Could I do that? Yes. But I don't trust my balance or my knees. So I fall. In fact, I practically leap. Just get me a soft, safe landing. Soon I'll need gymnastic crash mats covering my floors. If I ever have to move again it will only be to a bouncy castle.

"Life is like riding a bicycle. To keep your balance you must keep moving," Albert Einstein said. Wonderful advice. Until I lost trust in movement. These days, no movement is safe. Hills were made for walking downhill only. Walking up stairs can make me dizzy. Standing still is OK as long as it's not for too long. In fact, the only movement I do trust is riding my bicycle. Yoga, let's end this separation. Come back! I need you!

My unusable legs show up even when I'm swimming. I have a terrible kick. Mostly I just drag them behind me. Whether it's freestyle or backstroke my legs become logs, suspended from my waist to be towed to a distant but uncertain drop off. Every now and then I remind myself, "Oh yeah, kick!" So I'll do it for a while until my thoughts leave the pool and I swim in forgetfulness. Later I'll wonder, "What happened? Where did my legs go?" That's why I always end my workout with leg drills, doing a few laps holding the kickboard. It may amount to only 10% of my routine but it's something.

This is not a prescription for long-term physical well-being. Most studies show that keeping muscle strength and balance are essential for healthy aging. The torso won't survive long on its own without a stable and supportive trunk. Maybe this is why short people tend to live longer than tall people. They're much closer to the ground; their connection is more direct. If you think of legs as roots, they needn't extend far to support shorter people's upper branches. My legs need to go that much deeper. Instead, they seem planted in shallow, unstable soil, doomed to crumble in the next landslide and wash away to sea.

In one of my all-time favorite movies *WR: Mysteries of the Organism,* a Reichian therapist, a student of Wilhelm Reich himself, talks about how he always starts work with patients by staring at their complete, mostly unclothed bodies. That visual information is all he needs to begin. The physical body reveals a wealth of insight into someone's lifestyle and their habits, not just of body but of mind. In the film, he speaks to one example of a man who, well-muscled in his torso and arms, loomed large over thin, spindly legs. Though I watched the film repeatedly in my 20s, I never imagined that 45 years later he would be talking about me.

Being bow-legged doesn't help. Though the line from my hips to my knees is fairly straight, on the pilgrimage from my knees to my ankles my calves suddenly abandon ship to seek reunification with my knees. Striking out in opposite directions, they seem repulsed at moving in parallel. "I'm not going anywhere with *him*!" It's unclear which leg resents the other more. As a result, I walk around with my lower body shaped like a pretzel. To an artist's eye it may be aesthetically pleasing but any engineer will tell you it's not structurally sound. I'm hoping to become eligible for a body makeover like Rock Hudson got in the film *Seconds*.

Where this is headed, I don't know. Or rather, I do know—old age, sickness, and death. It's always good to know where you're going! This might be a good time to remember Alan Watts's dictum that the "I" is merely a term of reference to a momentary position in the world, a temporary viewpoint from which to perceive the passing parade. It's not a fixed position. It's a subjective point of view, fungible, ephemeral, no more than a passing attribute, evidence of nothing much. In short, I could sit and moan about it, or I can continue what I've already started—new workout exercises that include weights, leg strengthening, and balance. Maybe there's no changing room in the desert but there's certainly one at the gym!

CHAPTER ELEVEN

Ghosts Among Us

MY GIRLFRIEND'S STEPFATHER PETER moved to Puerto Rico after being diagnosed with dementia. He also has a bad back and bad feet, so he exercises by strolling at a snail's pace through the house with his cane. Around and around and around he goes. It's not a big house. Access and egress to the screened-in side porch, where anyone with any sense in Vieques spends most of the day underneath a large ceiling fan praying for a blow-through breeze, is only possible through two small bedrooms. So he'll often stop short when I'm on the bed struggling to put on my compression socks, wondering why a human is blocking his passage. In other places he likes to pause and ponder the imponderables. He stares for minutes over the front porch railing at the wonders of horses and iguanas in the yard. "Hmmm, I wonder who that is on the back porch doing yoga," he muttered one day. I looked. Turned out it was his daughter Jenny. He's not any clearer on who I am; perhaps since I'm already inside the house I'm presumed safe. After Franny, his wife of 50 years passed away, his curiosity led him to ask his son one day, "Did you know her well?"

In his circumambulations he often pauses at key junctions. One of his favorites is the side of the refrigerator where he gets to peruse the calendar. It may as well be the Rosetta Stone. Or maybe he's decoding the song of the ancient mariner. It represents all the meaning of the known universe. He pores over it to discern what might make today different from any other day. The sacred runes, though limited in import, point with clarity and directness: Blood test 9am. Aunt Elaine arrives 3pm. Lunch, Mama Mia, 1. This is not a DayMinder with multiple lines for numerous entries in a busy executive's schedule. It's your average Sierra Club giveaway, each month featuring a big photo of outdoor splendor, leaving only miniscule boxes for marking the day's activities. The implicit message is "What are you doing indoors anyway?" Maybe it's deciphering the small print that makes it such a challenge for Peter. He leans in carefully to extract every nuance he can from each phrase. What's guaranteed is that as soon as he leaves the kitchen and resumes his laps around the house, he'll forget it all, needing to return as soon as possible to genuflect once again before the altar of mystery. That works for a minute or two before one of his daughters happens by and he asks, "What are we doing today?"

After he dies, if he decides he wants to return and haunt the house it should be an easy transition. He need only resume following the path well-traveled. It's possible no one would notice. "Oh, that's just Peter. There he goes again, putting in his laps, still trying to figure out what the hell's going on. He died but doesn't know it." Family members with the misfortune to assume control of the house could become concerned as they might be unable to notice a practical difference. "Are you sure he's dead? Maybe we just assumed so when space suddenly opened up at the side of the refrigerator."

When made aware that Franny's sister Pippin had written a book, he became anxious to read it. What prompted him were likely my conversations with Jenny about the quality of the writing. The book had been lying around the house for weeks, yet he expressed no interest in it whatsoever. Once he understood that it concerned his wife's family, he got excited. So he started reading, but couldn't remember exactly why it was of interest. He knew there was a direct connection to his own life, but he was no longer sure what. "Who wrote it?" he asked his daughter Maggie one day. "Was she a former lover of mine?" She missed a great opportunity to reply, "Not unless you had an affair that none of us knew about Dad!"

Peter was also an alcoholic. He'd start drinking at noon every day and quit when he went to bed around 10. That was the pattern for most of his life. When his doctor insisted he make a change, Peter equivocated. Hey, it worked for 60 years, why change now? So Franny, an alcoholic herself, weaned him off vodka and tequila by insisting on wine. I suppose that's why he always took two ice cubes in his wine—the clinking served as a perfect sense memory, taking him back happily to the days spent drinking the harder stuff on the rocks. Transformed into a wino, when it came to reporting back to his doctor, Peter said, "I'm not drinking at all." After all the years of harder stuff that's not an unreasonable position to take. If he took a nap, he'd put the drink down by his bedside so he could resume his march to oblivion as soon as he woke up. Fortunately, he was a pretty good-natured drunk. Most of the time.

When Franny died, the children conspired to decrease his intake further. Drinking alone and averaging three bottles a day, he'd go through a case in four days. After buying a few days' allotment, someone would distract him while they poured out half of each bottle into an empty, and then re-fill them both with water. If Peter noticed the difference, he never said anything. Continuing the family ritual of eating lunch with other expats at a restaurant of choice somewhere on the island, the intrepid siblings made sure the bartenders were in cahoots. They too filled Peter's wine glass halfway with water. Maybe he himself no longer knew the difference. As long as the glass was always at hand and he could travel the elbow inflected journey to his mouth, he was fine. Based on his behavior, I'd say there's an unacknowledged upside to dementia: you can no longer tell whether you're drunk or not. Occasionally the siblings would find themselves in new eateries or have uninitiated friends pour him a full glass. This typically elicited a full-throated endorsement from Peter: "Man, this wine is *good*!"

The worst part of this experience was I found myself replicating both his physical demeanor and his behavior. I was becoming his unconscious mentee, a ghost in training. He clearly wasn't looking for an apprentice, but that choice wasn't his to make. I was standing ready, well suited for the job.

I have a curious tendency to imitate the mannerisms of people around me, everything from their physical movements, patterns of speech and accents, to their idiosyncratic behaviors. I attribute this chameleon-like instinct to my childhood narcissistic wounding. Pay careful attention to others lest you not receive their love for not being just like them! But I'm also a closet actor. I love inhabiting different roles to experience what life looks like from inside another pair of shoes. Arguably, this is the very root of my film work.

Around Peter, I found myself walking with an even slower, more unbalanced gait than usual, and taking on more confused and uncertain mental states. Not adapting well to the small, cramped house, I bumped into things regularly. Not sufficiently trained in orbiting the refrigerator calendar, I took to asking Maggie, sometimes with shocking regularity, "What are we doing today?" I grew confused when my Crocs were never to be found on the front porch where I left them the day before. Because it was later revealed that Maggie's son regularly borrowed them, I decided to hide them behind the door in our bedroom. This worked beautifully until I needed them again and completely forgot where they were. Instead, I testily texted her son to ask if he had absconded with them. I'm sure he took no small delight pointing out to me later that they were behind my own door. Following Peter's example, I was aging rapidly. With each passing day I was hurtling into senescence and decrepitude.

None of this was lost on Maggie. She remarked on how caring for Peter was good practice for what I might require of her in the future. For a relationship barely reaching its middle age—5.5 years together, the honeymoon worn off but the long-term rules of engagement not yet wholly negotiated—this was not encouraging news. I don't think prospects for happy stable relationships are ever built upon an edifice of one party becoming caretaker of the other, even if there is a 16-year age difference. "Honey, I love you so much I can't wait to push you around in a wheelchair! Sweetie, the prospect of exploring the woods with you on your walker is so exciting! My love, I look forward to bringing you Slurpee Pops and Juicy Juice on your deathbed." When we happened upon a house in Auburn, CA that we adored and ended up buying, I wasted no time developing jokes about how the strange anomaly of a built-in elevator would make it easy for Maggie to wheel me from the first floor to the second once I became wholly incapacitated.

Just because I was rapidly taking on Peter's behaviors, don't assume that every one of them was benign. I commonly got the death stare if I got to the refrigerator first and happened to be blocking his access when he wanted to refill his wine glass. Driving home from lunch one day he told me, "Stop the car! I want to get out." I assumed he urgently needed to pee, a circumstance I know well, until Jenny spoke up: "Dad, if you want him to drive slower all you have to do is ask. You don't need to get out of the car." Close encounters with death seemed to be lurking around every corner. Driving, especially at night, was always a risky undertaking. Should a car turn on to the road in front of us Peter would slap his hands on the dash and shout, "JEE-SUS!"

Apparently, there's a phenomenon common among the memory impaired called Sundowners Syndrome. The symptoms of dementia become stronger after sunset. It may manifest as confusion, impatience, paranoia, irritability and even violence. Other than outright violence, Peter exhibited all of these. Mostly it involved following his caregivers around like a faithful dog.

When the sun set, you had to watch out. Though I could rely on his irritability remaining restricted to only giving me the stink eye during the day, the evening hours could be volatile. When I reverted to the longstanding home habit of licking my plate after dinner, I grew concerned that he might lunge across the table and spear me with a fork. The waves of animosity were intense. Apparently a person with dementia may lose their ability to rationalize effectively, but good table manners never die.

For Peter, this problem was particularly acute with men. He seemed to have a plethora of unresolved father issues. Every man who came into his proximity represented untold danger requiring extreme caution. It didn't matter who it was—his own stepson and grandson were not to be trusted. Relative strangers like me were worse. I attributed it to his primordial relations with his own father who was a punitive and unforgiving man. Peter rebelled against every lesson his father had taught him. He hated him so much that after adolescence he never spoke to him again. A person more inclined to self-inquiry might have started therapy and discovered the residue of father issues in his own life and behavior. Instead, he took to drinking, becoming much like the father he abhorred.

His prospects for long-term survival are not good. He has congestive heart failure, A-fib and a very bad back. There's nerve damage down his leg so when he lifts it his foot flops forward. Hence, the cane. A long-time geriatric nurse who was a good friend gave him six months. Partly out of wishful thinking—his caretaking fell entirely to Jenny, Maggie, and their brother Gus, somewhat upending their lives—and partly for the relief that black humor can generate, Maggie started imagining him dying in different ways. Everyone assumed that part of his dying equation would be a broken heart over his late wife. Nobody counted on him not only *not* being stuck in grief but becoming excited at the prospect of new horizons. When I tell Maggie he might well live for another 10–20 years she groans.

It seems he has yet to receive the memo that he's supposed to die. He's fooled everyone and flourished. He's very much enjoying his new life in San Francisco, where both his daughters live—going to museums and exhibitions, taking walks to Dolores Park, relishing an array of fine, new restaurants—That wine is good! Increased sobriety may have a lot to do with it. His dementia may be getting worse, but he seems to be getting more clear-headed. Not all the local bartenders are in on the deal yet, but they soon will be. He may go to his grave the healthiest man he's been in years.

CHAPTER TWELVE

Sex Gurus Around the World

IN 1995 I DEVELOPED A TV SERIES with the title above. What follows are two paragraphs from the original proposal.

> "At once serious and whimsical, the series will focus on various scholars, thinkers, shamans, mystics, fakirs, tribal doctors, and high priests who have some special interest or expertise in sexuality. The series will exclusively cover non-Western thinking on the subject, whether nationally, ethnically, tribally, religiously, culturally, or mystically based. This is not *National Geographic* meets *Playboy* magazine. This is serious journalism treated with a lightness of touch, a joie de vivre, appropriate to any enlightened adult discussion of human sexuality. More like Paul Theroux travels with Dr. Ruth.
>
> The series will cover the globe, from small indigenous cultures like the Innuit in Northwestern Canada to the world's largest and longest-standing cultures like Hindu, Chinese, and Arab. By focusing each episode on a given person, the series will forefront human individuality and diversity. Idiosyncrasies of character will weave in and out of cultural history and biological theory to create a blend

of information and local color at once entertaining and informative—a celebration of multi-culturalism."

What led me to this idea was the work of Jolan Chang, particularly his first book published in 1977 called *The Tao of Love and Sex*. I ordered a copy before I finished reading the review in *Rolling Stone* magazine. I've since gone on to proselytize about its virtues to anyone who will listen.

In the wake of *Hoop Dreams'* success in 1994 I was casting about for new projects. This was one of many I pitched to agents and producers, talent scouts and production companies. I knew an episode on Jolan would be the perfect prototype episode. Again, from the proposal:

> "This year Jolan Chang will turn 80. A long-term resident of Stockholm, he doesn't like to travel much anymore because it's getting harder for him to find partners to make love with at least once a day, as is his custom. As a Taoist sex scholar, he offers himself as living proof of his ideas on health, aging, and human sexuality.
> The author of three books published in over 15 languages, and the subject himself of a book by Lawrence Durrell, the Taoist principles Chang espouses are basically these: 1) A man must learn to control and limit his ejaculation in order to make love as long, as frequently, and until any age he wishes, 2) Male orgasm is possible without ejaculation, 3) Women's complete satisfaction is essential for either partner to accrue health benefits from lovemaking."

I was always surprised that Jolan never became a household name, arriving as he did along with the second wave of feminism. HBO produced a weak half-hour episode for their *Real Sex* series which included scenes of Jolan in bed with his sex partner. I remember an interview in which she exclaimed his virtues as an attentive and skillful lover. I wasn't clear on the age differential between them, but

I guessed it was about 25 years with her in her 50s. She didn't strike me as attractive so that weakened my attention to the virtues of his ideas.

I'm not sure how I found Jolan's number, but I called him in Stockholm. I wanted his preliminary permission to film the premiere episode. He quickly agreed and we got to talking about other things, like how he expected to live well past 100. Soon we got around to discussing the frequency of my ejaculations. I explained that I had lost the discipline and motivation from my early 20s when I first read his book. He wasted no time in admonishing me. "You're 40 now and you will be dead by the time you are 80." I didn't take that too well. I wondered whether I shouldn't change the working title of that first episode to *Jolan Chang—Prophet of Doom*. His statement might have been responsible for me telling my financial planner 20 years later that I didn't expect to live past 80. As it turned out, Jolan himself died at 84 in 2002. I think he did his best to cover the fact of his death, because for years I couldn't get accurate information on how he was doing. Now I've changed my superannuation projections to 84.

That same year riding *Hoop Dreams*' coattails, I met Andrei Codrescu, the Romanian American writer and NPR commentator, at a party. He was touring with his own film *Road Scholar*, so I pitched him on a collaboration. "It's called *Sex Gurus Around the World* and…" "I'm in!" he replied before I got halfway through the sentence. He would've been the perfect on-camera foil for my diverse subjects—acerbic and skeptical, dryly funny and curious. At 77 he's still going strong and may well live longer than Jolan. As for me, getting to 84 might be pushing it. Jolan's prognostic curse may prove correct. Though too frequent orgasms remain a concern, at least I don't have to worry as much about ejaculation anymore. A completely useless TURP surgery—the roto rooter of the prostate—designed to relieve my Active Bladder Syndrome, did nothing at all to alleviate the urgent frequency of my need to pee but did take care of any future ejaculation concerns. No semen—no problem!

CHAPTER THIRTEEN

Living for Posterity

A FRIEND OF MINE ONCE SUGGESTED that the solution to all my PR, marketing, fundraising and distribution problems would be to have a documentary made about me. I thought it was a fine idea except for the drawback that there wasn't a soul in the world interested. No one was beating down my door to tell my life story. I floated the idea perhaps he would like to? Then I realized what a mistake that was given that he had no experience as a filmmaker. I certainly wasn't about to trust him with the telling of my story. Which raised a related issue. Who could make a film as good as I could?

I suppose I could make it myself, but the subject doesn't interest me. It's bad enough that I already write books that use myself as their principal subject. Somehow combining autobiographical anecdotes with mini-essays on contemporary subjects seems less vain than opening my life directly to cameras. But it's a fine line. You can spend a lot of time crawling up your own ass and saying, "My goodness, it's interesting in here!" Maybe it has to do with the medium itself. With the written word, putting my various neuroses up for examination and review and, hopefully, laughter, is one step removed. It's safer. Having that same scrutiny facing a camera would be too invasive. I'd be more self-conscious on camera and less willing to expose the same shortcomings that I write about with such enthusiasm. Not to mention the direct presence of a camera crew which, typically, is comprised of at least three people. A cadre of voyeurs peering into my every vulnerability in real time? No thank you.

Presumably, the intention behind a documentary on my life would be vastly different from the intention behind my books. A documentary designed to promote me would have to celebrate me. If someone showed up wanting to make *Frederick Marx: Fool or Idiot?* that's another issue. It's not that I'm categorically opposed to hagiography. I'd welcome it as an opportunity to get my movies and books more widely seen. It could prove a guarantor of posterity and produce real, tangible benefits. Michael Jordan paid millions of dollars to have *The Last Dance* made to secure his legacy as the GOAT—a piece of branded entertainment passing itself off as documentary.

You certainly couldn't make an exposé about my life. There's nothing left to expose. Sorry *60 Minutes*, my life is far too dull. I also can't qualify as an anti-hero; I'm too inoffensive. Irreverent? Yes. Offensive? I hope not. Investigative reporting would never uncover much since most of my offensiveness is saved for the inside of my skull. This book and my last aim to take some of that everyday dullness as a starting point and hold it aloft for comedy. It's the mundane minutiae of life, and my all-too-often neurotic responses to it, that fires my comic imagination.

But posterity as motivation can be hard to let go of. What to keep and what not to keep? All my projects represent a lot of hard work and a lot of reflection. The end product, whether film or book, is certainly not the only form the project takes while in development, and it may not even be the best. I'm proud of my work and even if it's not always celebrated, I like to retain a record of what went into it. It's important to be amused by and even delight in your own work. Otherwise, why do it? Becoming one more cynic discounting my own work is a disheartening way to live.

But when the task of preserving for posterity falls to me, I'm unreliable. I really struggle with what to keep and what to toss. Is it worthwhile to retain file drawers full of notes and releases and journals and article clippings that micro-document how a project was constructed? All the storyboards, production stills, press kits, journals, contracts, notebooks, press clippings, canceled checks? And what do you do with every form of film and video technology going back 50 years? 35mm film, 16mm film, 1", 2", 3/4," VHS, Beta, Beta SP, digital Beta, DV, mini-DV, DVDs, external hard drives, original field files, final master files… occasionally utilizing almost every format for a single film! Then multiply that by 20 films! Boxes and boxes of stuff. It's too much. Certainly no archive wants it and retaining it weighs me down.

Keeping one eye on future renown is not conducive to enjoying life in the present. It can become a form of living death to hold on to it all. I burned the 35mm negative from my half-million-dollar fiction film *The Unspoken* because every year when the bill for storage arrived it became yet another reminder of its commercial and artistic failure. Keep hope alive? Tell myself that you never know what might win favor in the future? Imagine it could be of use to a future biographer looking for minutiae about my life? You try living on those fumes of future success. I'd rather be a heroin addict.

Part of the problem is that stories about writers selling their archives surface regularly. I just read that Jhumpa Lahiri—though I respect her work, not exactly a household name, and at 57, still young—sold her "papers" to the NY Public Library. 40 linear feet worth of boxes. Who knows for how much. I was gratified to learn in 1994 that Allen Ginsburg sold his archive to Stanford University for $1 million. Despite the criticism he got in the press for not giving it away, I was relieved to know that he'd have some funds to continue to care for his 88-year-old live-in stepmother and hopefully a little left over to support himself into old age. (Unfortunately, he never quite got there and died at 70.) But money is not the issue. David Lynch donated his archives to the Academy Film Archive in 2007. What matters is knowing that the items have value to others.

The only reason I hung on for 30 years to some of the trophies, plaques, posters and awards I got for *Hoop Dreams* was the assumption that I would one day use them to furnish my Hollywood office. The importance of this practice was borne out to me while taking Hollywood meetings during those heady days. You want people in the waiting room to be impressed, even intimidated, at the prospect of meeting you. Somehow I missed out on that $10 million/5 picture deal, so the opportunity to stock my office with self-glorifying mementos never arose. Sans utility, there was no need to keep them. I did my best to punt on this decision by cramming all that swag into a friend's deep storage. But after 30 years it's safe to draw a few conclusions, so recently most of it got tossed.

And so it goes with all the personal stuff. Letters, mementos, flyers, and photos… who cares? I saved every one of my yearly event planners since the mid-1980s. Now of course there's online calendars, yet I still find it easier and more practical to carry an old-fashioned "analogue" datebook. I can't stand all that dinging and chiming, those so-called friendly reminders that are no less obtrusive than the silent ones, all the editing and rescheduling of appointments that take longer in the digital world than X-ing out one event and writing in another on an actual page of paper. Physical datebooks are convenient places to make notes, record data, and doodle. But what to do with them when the year is over? Call me crazy for lugging them from state to state but I've found they can come in handy. I've gone back to those books years later and found important data, most typically, a specific date when I accomplished a task, met someone, or had my head examined in a therapy session. But do I have that many *ongoing* uses for them? No. So what am I keeping them for exactly? After 40 years, I finally tossed them all.

Moving is the perfect time to test your posterity index. What objects do you want to bring with you into the remainder of your life and what objects is it time to leave behind? It forces you to get real about what you keep for practical use and, that ever-present nagging question, what you hope people will discover once you're gone. It's a reality check. Still investing energy in the vain hope people will recognize your genius when you're dead? God help you. What I hope people will discover when I'm gone is that I wasn't an asshole leaving behind mountains of shit for them to sort through and toss. That's motivation. That's love!

CHAPTER FOURTEEN

Get Out of the Pool!

SWIMMING IS MY FAVORITE FORM OF EXERCISE. But don't try to throw me in the ocean or any large body of water. Lakes, bays, inlets… all too big for me. I prefer the safe confines of chlorinated pools with clearly marked lanes and walls to push off. Especially those with a nearby hot tub.

For years I swam in a very small pool at a downtown Oakland health club. Three narrow lanes, each without adequate space for two people to share. 3 lanes + 3 people = max capacity. I made a point of arriving mid-morning or mid-afternoon when typically there were few others. Occasionally, due to bad timing or bad luck, the lanes were full and I had to wait or give up on swimming for the day.

One day, while waiting for a lane, I found myself ruminating on this issue, wondering why I had the misfortune to be left out. Why is it that on certain days people always want to swim when I do? Imperfect timing? What creates this misfortune? Was it bad karma? A conspiracy? Why do others interfere with my schedule?

Once I got in and started my laps, I noticed other people had come in. Now they too were waiting for lanes. At first I felt assured, justified even, enjoying my lane. I typically swim for about 40 minutes—get in, swim 40 laps and get out. I don't lollygag. But given the circumstances—a small, lone pool in a large downtown area—my awareness suddenly flipped on me, and I questioned whether taking that much time was appropriate. I started imagining the monologues going through the minds of the people waiting. "What is it with this guy? Why does he take so long? Can't he see people are waiting?" I assumed their thoughts to be similar to my own: "What created my misfortune? Was it bad karma? Less than perfect timing? A conspiracy? Why do others interfere with *my* schedule?" I saw myself from their imagined perspective. I was the problem. The pool was crowded because I was still in it. I was taking up space, denying others a chance. I thought, "Maybe it's time for me to get out of the pool." It was an epiphany. (OK, I still finished my laps, but I didn't dilly-daddle!)

I had a similar experience of awareness suddenly doing a back flip on me when I was in graduate school. I was serving on the graduate student council, representing the department of cinema and photography. The student head of the film programming committee came to us for approval of funds for weekend student center film showings. Typically, this event was pro forma. I started quizzing him on why they didn't show more foreign and independent films—more "adult fare"—alongside the popular Hollywood films. He replied reasonably that graduate students also attended the more commercial films and in fact, the committee did occasionally program more challenging fare. Still, I persisted. Having been a programmer myself I found it disappointing that more experimental work wasn't regularly on offer, stretching students' vocabulary of cinematic expression. Growing frustrated, the young man threw up his hands and said, "Look. We're only asking for $500." Naturally, I had a rejoinder to that. But mid-sentence the room inexplicably flipped on me. I suddenly realized that no one else particularly cared about the issue much less shared my concern; I was grinding my own ax. Worse, I was being an asshole. Time to let this go. And I did, much to the relief of the student programmer and the rest of the council. But that sudden experience of the room turning inside out never left me. Of course, friends long familiar with me are no strangers to me being an asshole.

We never see ourselves as part of the problem. Holding up funding, taking up extra legroom on flights, making the line longer at the grocery store, adding to the traffic jam… Consider it one of the many byproducts of our individualistic society. Being in it for #1 is just the way we roll. But the problem isn't someone else, it's us!

You might try a simple thought experiment sometime, wherever you are, whatever you're doing: "What is my presence, right here, right now, doing to impact others? How am I affecting *their* day? Am I getting my own needs met while others be damned? While not discounting those needs can I make some adjustment to better accommodate others? Can I compromise?"

I experienced a similar revelation about the necessity of bending my own standards to those of the greater community while riding my bicycle in Tianjin, China in the early 1980s. At that time, bicycles ruled, probably outnumbering cars 100:1. The only traffic jams I saw were caused by bicycles. Initially I was too intimidated to ride. To wait for a space to ease into traffic was foolish. There were no spaces. You simply had to merge as deftly as possible with the oncoming rush and let others accommodate you. It was like entering a river. The water doesn't stop to allow your body to get oriented. You push off and instantly you're floating along at the same speed. Nothing made me feel more a part of Chinese society, like I belonged. Nothing in their society seems designed to accommodate you and you alone, yet somehow everyone gets accommodated.

And so it goes with the planet. It moves along at its own pace in its own cycles. None of the natural forces pause to accommodate any of us—weather, seasons, aging or dying. In our unconsciousness, in our individualism and consumptive thinking, we accelerate degrading those forces by rapaciously exploiting natural resources and expelling pollutants. There are limits to how the earth can accommodate us, and we're beginning to experience some—fewer trees for fuel, shelter and oxygen, shrinking supplies of fresh water, depleted stocks of fish, disappearing topsoil for growing food, flora and fauna extinction. Carbon, the master of the economy, required for everything, even making solar panels, electric cars, and windmills, will run out. Unless we re-tune to those natural cycles that can provide unceasing, though not unlimited, bounty, spaceship Earth only has so much to go around, and time is running out.

That's why many young people feel frustration with us boomers. We came of age in a time of economic expansion and consumer abundance. We achieved the highest standard of living for the greatest number of people in the planet's history. We're used to helping ourselves to whatever we want; we feel entitled to it. With a global population of 8+ billion now, it's time for us to get out of the pool. No, I'm not suggesting mass euthanasia. I'm suggesting we have to be conscious of the time we have left, the ways that we use it, and shift our focus away from our own needs to the needs of the collective, to the others waiting. Right now, at least seven generations are watching us from the future. Let's get them in the pool and give them a chance at a good swim.

CHAPTER FIFTEEN

Lost in Translation: More China Follies

EPISODE 1

MY ADVENTURE WITH JOCK ITCH began not long after my arrival. I figured some common ointment would do the trick, but I was so embarrassed by my condition that I refused to ask the Waiban, the Office of Foreign Affairs, to accompany me to the clinic of our work unit. (Truth be told, I had developed a crush on the woman who served under Director Wang, so she was the last person I wanted to ask.) I certainly could've asked Wang himself, but I was unsure about discussing my genitals with a university administrator. In China at that time it might not have been politically incorrect to have jock itch, but for this capitalist roader it certainly was cause for shame.

So I went to the clinic myself. My Mandarin at that time consisted largely of "How are you?" (colloquially, "Have you eaten?") and "Yes, I'm a foreigner." (colloquially, "Yes, I have a big nose."). When it became clear that I was there for a medical issue, I met their questions by scratching my toes. I figured toe fungus was likely similar to whatever was ailing my balls so whatever they prescribed would probably work. To their curious and detailed questions, their increasing perplexity, I relentlessly pantomimed scratching my toes and foot. When they made it clear I should take off my shoes and socks to show them, I acted even more stupidly than I was already behaving by pretending I didn't understand. Had they examined my toes carefully they quickly would have determined they were happy and well-adjusted. To their complete consternation, I kept scratching at my shoe like a mime with Tourettes. Finally, my idiocy exhausted them, and they gave me my reward—a bottle of some dark, tinted potion. They pantomimed applying it liberally every day. They might even have demonstrated the sun going across the sky.

When those doctors reported back to the Waiban later, as they surely must have given my inexplicable arrival at their office without escort, they probably said, "It's probably just jock itch. But since he didn't bother to bring a translator, who gives a shit when his balls light on fire."

And so they did. To this day I have no clue what chemicals went into the paint remover I brushed liberally on to my testes, but I spent the subsequent half hour each day hopping from foot to foot and fanning my balls. If anyone ever puts your balls in a vise and tightens the jaw with a hammer, you'll have a fair approximation of what I experienced. Perhaps I should have taken the more direct route and simply applied gasoline and lit them on fire.

It took an hour or two for the pain to wear off. I watched in horror as the skin writhed and rippled like an alien giving birth to a monster child. Scabs formed the next day. Like a snake shedding its skin, by the third day sheets of burned and dry skin peeled off. Fortunately, I'm red/green color blind so I really couldn't tell how pink and raw the underlying skin was. The temporary relief from pain meant only one thing—time for another liberal application. No pain, no gain. Nothing if not a determined experimenter with my own body, (see *My Life as a Lab Rat*) I did this for weeks. I don't recall if it actually removed the originally offending jock itch. The inability to feel anything there at all likely took away any lingering memory of irritation. It's a miracle that in subsequent years I still managed to produce semen. That is, until my needless TURP surgery 40 years later (see *Sex Gurus Around the World*).

Episode 2

I LEARNED HOW TO ANTAGONIZE AUDIENCES with my very first film. *Dream Documentary* (1980), a five-minute experimental collage, was comprised of rapid-fire shots stitched together from found footage—old 16mm movie miscellany rescued from my mentor Ron Epple's attic, otherwise destined to be put out in the next day's garbage. Included were old newsreels from the 50s, a *Twilight Zone* episode, the 1956 Michigan State football season, and some long outdated educational films. My film was not meant to tell a story but was meant as a comment on filmmaking itself; how images get used, particularly by Hollywood filmmakers and TV news to promote an unspoken ideological agenda. One film critic argued that the lone shot taken from a homemade porn film was out of place and irrelevant.

Though the film won awards at small festivals, I had yet to screen it outside the rarified air of film cognoscenti. Home for the summer before moving to China, I learned of a conference for political activists taking place on campus. Never having considered myself an activist, I nonetheless felt ideologically aligned so I promptly arranged for all three of my newly minted films to be shown. "The perfect audience!" I thought. I xeroxed ten copies of a handwritten notice announcing the showing of "Free Political Films!" and posted them in hallways outside the meeting rooms.

Things got off to a fiery start. "Why do you call these films 'political?'" someone shouted from the back of the hall. Almost 40 years prior to its official arrival, I had a direct experience of being canceled by woke culture. *Dream Documentary* was first up. Audience members accused me of presenting North Vietnamese soldiers as bloodthirsty killers. The activists took the reassembled images purely on face value; all subtleties were lost in the translation to the new context. Ideologically driven leftists clearly were not destined to become my ideal audience. Maybe my films didn't have enough comrade farmers singing and dancing with pitchforks and shovels. Consider it my first lesson in screening films: the meaning of the film is a time and place equation. Ultimately it is not the product of the mind of the filmmaker, but created in the minds of viewers. The scourge of ideological purity left its boot print on my sensitivities and helped crystallize my emerging self-understanding as an artist. Clearly I was not a revolutionary.

Soon I was antagonizing audiences on both sides of the Pacific. Six months after screening my films for leftists in the US, I screened them for Chinese Communist Party officials at Tianjin University. In order to be allowed to present them to students, colleagues, friends and faculty, I had to screen them for local party members first. Subtleties and ambiguities, I quickly learned, don't find much favor anywhere. This was all arranged by the Waiban head Wang.

Wang wasn't an academic. Like many risen to administrative ranks in those days he had modest roots from a small town in central China. If he was not a Communist Party member himself, it was safe to assume he regularly reported to one. What he lacked in intellectual depth he made up for in craftiness. He bartered my services to others. I'm sure he got a nice kickback when I added a second job to my main responsibilities of teaching ESL to sophomores by also lecturing off campus once a week at Tianjin Teachers College to secondary school English teachers on the subject of modern British Literature—a subject I knew nothing about. What it might have taught my students I can't say, though they quickly educated *me* on issues like the caprice of communist administrative practice. More than a few, having taught Russian their entire lives and never spoken a word of English, were transferred into my class a week before school began. What they understood of my lectures aside from hello could itself be the subject of a Gogol novel.

Wang also served as my translator the day I lectured on contemporary film theory at the Tianjin Film Studio. Have you ever had an experience of giving a public talk in a foreign country when your appointed translator clearly doesn't understand a word you're saying? That day in Spring 1984 it happened to me. Admittedly, I was using a lot of academic jargon even American college students struggle with: phenomenology, semiotics, Lacanian psychoanalysis, eidetic. But I made a point of preparing Wang beforehand, giving him mini-lectures on those terms and others, including feminism and the male gaze. It didn't matter. It all went over his head. I'll never forget the faces of the young studio workers. Initially excited to be introduced to new ideas, I watched them grow increasingly perplexed and disappointed as my lecture went from surreal to painful. Though my command of Chinese was minimal at the time, I can remember sentences sounding like, "If you consider the thing I was talking about earlier and compare that to the thing I was talking about before you'll see that they pretty much agree overall with what I'm saying."

My record of confusing people with highfalutin ideas had a proud and distinguished history. Four years earlier at Southern Illinois University I gave a talk on Marxist Film Theory to a class of undergraduates. Nearing the end of my 50-minute lecture a student raised his hand and asked, "Now let me get this straight. This system is named after you? These are *your* ideas?" When most of the class finished laughing, I calmly explained that in the mid-1800s there was this guy named Karl Marx and that he and I were of no known relation. In Communist China you might expect to find ease and facility in understanding Marxism and its application to film. But I doubt Wang Sheng was any more familiar with dialectics than my clueless SIU-C student, nor was he any more prepared to not make sweeping assumptions than college revolutionaries were.

Though *Dream Documentary* contained no spoken language, transcripts of my other films were produced in advance for the Tianjin University Party officials. I prayed they were not written by Wang. When the screening date arrived, he was there, prepared to take credit for the miracles of my creativity should things go well, equally prepared to throw me under the bus if they didn't. Trying to forestall another train wreck, I apologized for *Dream Documentary* in advance, doing my best to explain the film. That effort in itself would have made for a nice comic short—explaining what experimental film is to Communist Party officials, many without high school education, only six years after the Cultural Revolution ended. Even milquetoast Hollywood films were considered seditious during those insurrectionary days.

In a rare demonstration of international solidarity, Chinese Communist cadres agreed with my state-side film critic. The homemade porn shot was deemed irrelevant, sufficient to disallow the film for screening. Fortunately, the CP brass deemed the other films acceptable. I was surprised to learn just how acceptable. Since my film *House of UnAmerican Activities* details persecution that my parents experienced in the 1950s by virtue of their membership in the Communist Party USA, the Chinese were in fact keen to screen it. In the Chinese pantheon of heroism, experiencing martyrdom at the hands of a foreign government ranked high. I was suddenly elevated in stature—a minor Communist star. It had never occurred to me to spotlight my Communist DNA and receive fringe benefits. For my remaining year in China, I quite likely could have commanded more privilege and risked outrageous behavior and presumed to get away with it all. My Communist fame proved short-lived though, as my film *Dreams from China,* released four years later, critiqued China's human rights record, no doubt tanking any of my remaining star status and making me wary of re-entering China anytime soon. Proof yet again that it is only a matter of time until I antagonize everyone.

I don't recall any of these thoughts going through my head a year later when I approached the cultural attaché of the US embassy in Beijing to also screen my films. He pre-screened them and pronounced them suitable for the public. When I pointed out to him that the film on my dad didn't make the US government look very good, he calmly replied that it was fine; it showed that we can make mistakes and that we tolerate dissent. I confess to flushing with a rare sense of pride in my own country at that moment. They screened *Dream Documentary*, homemade porn shot and all.

EPISODE 3

THE POP BAND WHAM! lay claim to being the first Western band to tour China. I'm here to set the record straight. They were not. I know because three months before they arrived in April 1985, I traveled with the band that was. Documenting that trip was the greatest film I never made. It could have done more for my career than Hoop Dreams.

Licensing the outtakes alone might have netted tens of thousands of dollars.

My Canadian friend Will Goede, an English professor at the same university where I worked in Beijing, was a saxophone, clarinet, and flute player. He loved jazz, his bona fides dating back to the 40s touring with Big Bands. He was the old man, the godfather in a group of eight that otherwise averaged about 24 years old. David, the only American, was the principal organizer and songwriter. He put the band together from expat contacts in Beijing. Only he and Will were residents at the Friendship Hotel where I also lived. Their self-chosen name was Beijing Underground. But when an enterprising Chinese promoter heard them and conjured up waterfalls of cash, he signed them to a management deal, insisting, for political reasons, they change their name to Mainland Band.

What a polyglot of international talent! Paul, the bass player, was Tunisian. Two others were from Zaire, doing guitar and vocals, bringing with them the popular brand of soukous music which originated in Congo. Two more were from Madagascar and the last, a Palestinian, was a retired sergeant from the PLO, having picked up his percussion skills as a bazooka specialist.

The promoter proposed a ten-city tour through south China during the winter holiday. Per my winter norm, I was sick in mid-December. A French journalist from *Paris Match* magazine said he'd been commissioned to write a story. He also said he was negotiating for funds to make a documentary. From my sickbed, I told him I'm your guy.

My girlfriend and I packed our bags and joined the band for the train ride south. Settling into our cabin, I remember Pierre remarking on what a different impression I made in good health, standing tall, wearing my black leather jacket. The jacket especially seemed to impress him. Maybe stereotypes about French fashion are true.

Since forthcoming money was promised, I didn't think to bring my Super 8 camera that I was using for my own film *Dreams from China*, nor to borrow my friend George's 16mm Bolex. It was only later that the news came down that there was to be no funding.

The first gig was in Shenzhen, the newly designated "Special Economic Zone" not far from Hong Kong. The city was deserted, the scene of a neutron bomb explosion. I remember huge avenues with few cars and fewer bicyclists—an inexplicable rarity in China—and skyscrapers with no one going in or out. Access to the city was strictly regulated, presumably to protect civilians from exposure to too much capitalism. In the 40 years since, this former fishing village has been transformed into a paragon of "socialism with Chinese characteristics"—more commonly understood as capitalist dictatorship.

The *di-si-ke*—the three character transliteration for disco—was at the end of one of those broad, empty avenues. The dance floor alone could accommodate 500. On each of the three nights of concerts I remember there being maybe 25 in attendance. In order to make myself useful, I found my way to the unmanned sound booth. There, at my disposal, were a mixing panel and a lighting effects switcher. Having had experience mixing sound for my own films, I did my best to isolate the sources for mics and instruments, boosting the vocals when I could, dropping back bass and drums. The lighting effects were another matter. I bathed the band in alternating waves of blue, red, and yellow, experimenting as I tried to learn the system, occasionally strobing them in purple during a somber love song. None of it mattered. The empty cavern produced the show stopping results to be expected. I don't recall if people even danced.

The Guangzhou concerts were altogether different. A tiny nightclub on the top floor of an elite hotel, the much smaller venue became a pressure cooker with explosive results. Like Shenzhen, access was automatically limited to the extremely well connected—largely the sons and daughters of Chinese communist officials. Unlike Shenzhen, the stage was a mere foot above the dance floor with a small mixing panel off to the side. There couldn't have been more than 30 in the audience.

Didn't matter. As soon as the first chords were struck, the crowd was delirious. I witnessed them being introduced to their own human bodies, maybe for the first time. They weren't dancing. They were spasmodically erupting. Thirty-five years of communist rule and regulation exploded out of their bodies. They were suddenly liberated from all social strictures, discovering the full range of human physical expression in real time. If ever I questioned the riotous, absolutely subversive power of rock 'n roll, this first night put my doubts to rest.

Maybe average workers wouldn't have comprehended what was on offer, much less afforded themselves license to experience it. Maybe those elites knew what they could get away with. In any case, their rational minds took a quick and well-deserved vacation. They became ecstatically unhinged, a frenzied mob. That's when my job description shifted from sound mixer to bouncer. Young men, not content to jump onstage and dance, tried to seize the instruments from the musicians. When I grabbed them and threw them offstage, they climbed back up, throwing themselves bodily at band members. This was real rock 'n roll—the Sex Pistols performing *Anarchy in the UK* in Manchester in December 1976, the whole room a mosh pit. I had never witnessed anything like it. Stupefied with wonder, I worried that my friends might be torn to shreds.

On the day before the last performance, there was a sit-down meeting with the band. As usual, the promoters were not present, but word came down that gigs were not materializing as expected, and that funds were not forthcoming. It didn't take long to scrutinize the dead weight. Pierre had long since absconded to Paris with his story. My girlfriend Heli was considered expendable despite the wonderful photographs she was taking. My services as sound mixer, lighting director, and bouncer were deemed irrelevant. Not taking issue; we couldn't really claim to be anything other than freeloaders. Heli got the next day's train to Beijing while I went to Hong Kong for a few days, got sucker-punched by a shopkeeper when I got angry at him cheating me, pressed charges and collected a small amount of settlement cash outside the municipal courtroom, then flew to the Philippines to cool out for a week on the beach. Back home in Beijing, friends enjoyed reading the little story about me in the China Daily.

The band survived and went on without us. They played a few more gigs in the south before the tour itself collapsed and they all went home. A few one-off concerts surfaced in the spring—one in Wuhan or Xian—along with some local ones. They performed at a dance at UIBE—the school where Will and I worked. I turned my video team out to film it and one not wholly successful dolly shot ended up in the promotional video I made for the university. The band also performed in the main building of our Friendship Hotel complex. That was particularly heady as I got to add doorman to my rock and roll manager resumé and decide which of the dozen or more young people who showed up late should get in. The hottest event in Beijing that night, that week, that month, the barroom was packed with over 100 bodies writhing to the music. Twenty years after its arrival in the US, my international friends and colleagues got to experience for themselves what Beatlemania looked like, imported to China.

Though the band professionally recorded two audio cassettes which were distributed with no discernible marketing plan, other promised dates were not fulfilled, money was never transparently or equally dispersed, and the whole thing collapsed by summer. If anyone could ever publish the story and get half the truth told, I'm sure the bandmates or the promoter would have best sellers. Sadly, my beloved friend Will, who was a professional writer along with being a professor and musician, never wrote about it and now has dementia. Hence, the many unknowns in this telling. As it is, what survives of the band are only those two tapes featuring about 12 songs, with sleeves containing multiple photos, along with some 3/4" raw video footage likely long since forgotten or erased in UIBE's vault. But I'm here to tell you, with Will's mighty saxophone blasts chain-sawing through a refined three guitar melodic wall like the E Street Band's Clarence Clemons, African rap, scat-like, dulcet vocals sailing in from every quadraphonic quarter, and propulsion from a battery of north African percussion, *that band could rock*!

Unlike Wham! who played only two concerts in China—a small one in Guangzhou and one in Beijing at the People's Gymnasium for an audience of 12,000 which included Heli and me. The band's opening act DJ Trevor did put the fans into a frenzy as they went dancing into the aisles. Proving once again that when the people are ready to rock not even the quality of the music will deter them. Unfortunately, a police state will. The authorities quickly shut it all down, announcing during the break that no more standing, clapping, or dancing would be tolerated. Given the hundreds of uniformed police standing ready to pounce from every aisle, their proscription proved effective. Little matter, as Wham's music soon performed its own soporific miracles by putting everyone to sleep. As I later opined in my film *Dreams from China*: "Comrades, this wasn't even rock 'n roll! Now here's the real thing, here's The Clash!" As apropos as it was, I ended up not using the Clash song *Police on my Back* in the film, and sadly, I never found a way to put any of Beijing Underground's music in there either. But at least I got to witness them at their rock 'n roll apex, cutting like a buzzsaw through the fabric of Chinese culture.

CHAPTER SIXTEEN

Why I Will Never Be Politically Correct

MOST PEOPLE DON'T KNOW that the term *politically correct* originates with the Communist Party. When the Communists seized power in Russia in 1917 and inaugurated the Union of Soviet Socialist Republics, they became the masters of the worldwide communist movement. Communist Parties everywhere, whether part of the USSR or not, served the dictates of the Central Committee in Moscow. Communists everywhere were supposed to follow the official party line on every issue. Whether the topic was "What caused the global depression?" "What caused mass starvation in Ukraine?" "The Woman Question," or "What to do about race relations in the US?" there was always an official answer traceable back to Moscow. Every Party member was expected to recite some version of that explanation. That's how politically correct took root in the English language, becoming common usage among CP-USA members in the 1930s. To do other than follow the official line was to be deemed politically *in*correct and risk expulsion from the Party, which, strange as it may seem, carried some real weight with members. Consider it analogous to devout Catholics being excommunicated from the Church.

Did those staunchly anti-fascist Communists do some serious pirouetting in 1939 when Stalin signed a non-aggression pact with Hitler? You bet. Suddenly the world's poster child for fascism became "The good friend of the Soviet people." Stalin trusted Hitler and so this preposterousness became the politically correct position, and

Communists everywhere parroted the stance. This only created greater whiplash when, less than two years later, Hitler had the bad sense to attack the USSR, thereby sealing his country's ultimate fate in WWII. Much to the relief of Communists everywhere, "Nazis are now the enemy" became politically correct overnight. You might be wondering: Why can't dictators just get along?

I was 18 when I first learned that my mother and father had been members of the Communist Party. Looking through family albums on our living room couch with my girlfriend one day I discovered articles from the *Philadelphia Enquirer* about my father's appearance before HUAC—the House Committee on UnAmerican Activities. That was 1956, when I was nine months old.

Discovering my parents' secret history suddenly threw light on an experience I knew but couldn't name, something unspoken and hidden at the center of things. The facts alluding to this mystery were self-evident but never discussed: Why did we seldom see our extended family? We scarcely knew our grandparents, uncles and cousins. Why did my mother speak darkly about mail being opened or never delivered? Why did she get phone calls from people who wouldn't say anything and then hang up? Dark forces seemed to be lurking, and an unnamed fear seemed to drive some of my parents' decisions. Later I learned that my father had been blacklisted as a waiter and HUAC had threatened him with deportation. No wonder.

They quietly left the Party not long thereafter, not because of my dad's inability to get work or the threats from HUAC, but because of Nikita Khrushchev. That same year, at the 20th Party Congress in Moscow, the Soviet Premier denounced Stalin and admitted that the dictator had in fact "… made a few mistakes." Once the news of that admission spread to Communists worldwide, and eventually to the public, my parents quietly abandoned the Party along with the vast majority of CP members. Vast Soviet gulags and the KGB's 30-year reign of terror were not mentioned by name or in detail; they were inferred. And it didn't help that mere months later the Soviets crushed the Hungarian revolution. My parents were forced to acknowledge that at least some of the capitalist propaganda they had heard all their lives from US media was in fact true. Talk about irony. The very year my father was persecuted and blacklisted for being a communist they learned that their own belief in Soviet communism was a mistake, itself based on propaganda. It's hard to imagine how my parents so thoroughly deluded themselves. Yet there they were, brilliant nonconformists, conforming to views dictated by Moscow.

My siblings and I grew up after these storms had largely passed. To their credit, my parents never insisted that we assume some particular political point of view, certainly not that we become communists. Though we discussed politics regularly and they always expressed profound empathy for working people, poor people, immigrants and people of color—the salt of the earth—we were never directed to any particular ideology or way of thinking. They never discussed their political past with us because they wanted to protect us from potential abuse, the ostracizing we might receive from teachers and peers. We were encouraged to think for ourselves, to look, consider deeply and analyze by our own measure. They parsed what were commendable morals and values from anything that smacked of the totalistic, systemic and ideological. (That is, until my mother discovered feminism!) A proud member of this tradition, I stand here today as the Marx rebel du jour, at your service, more Groucho than Karl.

Recent waves of political correctness washing over contemporary culture leave me nauseous. Of course, the people who insist on political correctness never use that term. But political correctness has become a fact of life for both the Right and the Left; cancel culture operates on both sides. Just as the Right attacks and devours its own fellow travelers for anything less than ideological purity, even if merely the conspiracy theory of the day, so does the Left. On the Right, they say they're *protecting freedom*. They just do it by trying to inhibit the freedom of others. On the Left, they use *woke* or *time's up* or some other hot button slogan to denounce someone with a perceived misstep or shortcoming. They forge justice by denying justice to those accused. Because of someone's momentary indiscretion or use of a particular word, phrase, image, or sound they can be branded racist, sexist, homophobic, or of propagating some other ism. The "correct line" may no longer be coming from Moscow, but ideologues of the world unite to forge new ones. I'm having déjà vu all over again!

I think it's the nature of the young to want to poke a finger into the eye of elders. I certainly did. But assuming the high ground of political correctness never serves to create a just world. Hounding people out of public office, a role in media, a university administrative post, or a civil service job because of their politics, or worse, a single bad choice they made, really tells us more about the accusers than the accused. By claiming the ground of the righteous, both the Left and the Right prove the limitations and dangers of the self-righteous. While they signal their high-minded virtue, both sides demonstrate a breathtaking lack of understanding or compassion. By claiming victim status, both sides become perpetrators, doxxing opponents, branding people guilty until proven innocent. These perpetrators then start witch hunts, spreading vitriol both within and outside their own ranks, *othering* everyone. Wise Elders, voices of more reasoned judgment and compassion, of deep listening, get cast aside. In the end, both sides end up purging their own ranks if anyone steps out of line, simultaneously dismissing all outsiders who don't fall into lockstep. And so it goes. Two different standards of political correctness, however divergent from each other, demand making universal enemies of anyone who chooses not to accept them. You must kowtow to the known standards of your nearest in-group or risk exile.

It's a challenge for free-thinkers like me. As an artist, some presume to take away my right to make films about people different from me. My creative task, as I've long seen it, is now supposed to be of little value—to put myself in the shoes of subjects to learn as much as I can about how the world looks and works from their vantage point. That's what artists do; we shape-shift to discover truths in the world around us. Since political correctness tells me I can't really know what it's like to be gay or lesbian, an African American, a welfare recipient, an immigrant, a prisoner, a Veteran, homeless, or even a young person, I should stop making films about them all. Poof! There goes 45 years of filmmaking! All my instincts, not to mention all of Buddadharma, tell me that when I meet the Other, there go I in another form. I carry a responsibility not only to empathize, but to honor and protect them. To betray that obligation is to deny the moral virtue of every value taught me by my parents. That I will not do.

Meanwhile, all sides clamor for greater victim status. It's the Victim Olympics—a race to the winner's circle of Most Aggrieved. Faced with this stark reality, a dark symbolic vision landed in my mental inbox. Picture burning tar sands of hell with hundreds of open mouths, extended arms with stricken hands reaching skyward, frenzied to receive release from their suffering:

> I'm the victim here.
>
> No, I'm the victim. I have it unbelievably bad!
>
> I have it worse! I'm the victim!
>
> My victimization is greater than all of yours!

This is the seemingly universal state of desperation we presently inhabit, Left, Right and even some of the Center. For me, every ideology is equally suspect, including multiculturalism. None of them can take into account the uniqueness of circumstance for every single person, place or time. In effect, they are theories. Theories can be useful for helping make sense of the world, but only to a point. They are never universal, never eternal, never unconditioned. Like all mental constructs there is no irreducible substance to them. Ephemeral as wisps of smoke, there is no *there* there. As Hannah Arendt once said: "The self-compulsion of ideological thinking ruins all relationship with reality."

So please, can we all stop playing "Gotcha!" with each other? Before doling out verdicts, before branding someone as incorrect, can we first listen deeply and try to understand where they're coming from, what their deepest intentions are for what they say or do? They might still be wrong; we might still need to take issue with them. Fine. But if we can do it from a place of compassion then maybe we have a chance to build a bridge over the one river that flows through us all, rather than poison it and eliminate what our mutual survival requires us to drink.

CHAPTER SEVENTEEN

I Love My Friends. I Think.

HAVE YOU EVER LOOKED AROUND at your friends and wondered "How did this happen? How did I get to be friends with these people?" My guess is that thought never pops into most people's heads. If that's true for you, great. Of course for me, taking Socrates' dictum to the extreme that the unexamined life is not worth living, that thought about friends pops into my head regularly. Why doesn't anyone talk about how the *over*examined life is the handmaiden to neurosis? Who the hell lives by the maxim "Examining your life relentlessly might clarify what ails you but it's a guarantee to rack up your therapy bills?"

When I was young, I used to imagine living in New York or LA surrounded by a social network of brilliant artists, musicians and writers. Let's group them together and call them Deep Creatives. I trust them. They're truth-tellers. Unlike most people, they don't have axes to grind, positions to protect, agendas to manifest. They're about making art, expressing themselves to jolt people into thinking in new ways. Certainly there were times in my adult years when I did reside in NY and LA and had experiences like that.

I even had a limited version of that experience in college, both my undergraduate and graduate days, though not in places like NY or LA. We're talking the universities of Champaign-Urbana and Carbondale, Illinois, not popularly recognized hotbeds of innovative thought, given their image in the broader culture as part of the flyover zone. But in the 1960s, Carbondale hosted Buckminster Fuller and a raft of famous writers while Champaign became seminal in the creation and development of computer technology and home to multiple Nobel and Pulitzer Prize winners, along with Harry Partch, John Cage and Chungliang Al Huang. My own friends at that time, though few called themselves artists, were brilliant in their own ways, and funny. They certainly qualified as Deep Creatives. The fact that I no longer seem to be surrounded by people like that is clearly my own fault. Was it insecurity that drove me elsewhere? What happened?

Maybe not feeling as stimulated by your friends is a function of age and only worsens as you get older. Younger people tend not to concern themselves with this question. Friends organically evolve, you get along, have fun, discuss revolution, sex and quantum physics; what's to worry? When you get older you want more stability, calm and ease in your life. Most people tend not to look for the fireworks of Big Ideas, the impetus for dramatic action. Your days of wanting to jump up from the dinner table and knock down a wall with a friend—which is what happened one evening when a guest suggested we expand the kitchen on my friend Carole's farm—are behind you. But I enjoy stuff like that even today. I welcome a conversation over a meal that suddenly veers from grazing in exciting pastures of thought into taking quick action.

Maybe it's inertia. The older and more set in my ways I get, the less I seek new friends to engage in deep speculative and philosophical conversations. I have my work. I enjoy the company of my girlfriend. I largely stay home where my social life is confined to reading or watching an evening movie.

You might think it's a function of place. The truth is you can find Deep Creatives pretty much everywhere. I know a brilliant sculptor who lives in Louisville, Kentucky. Having spent time in Southern Illinois on the farm with Carole and her newly expanded kitchen, I knew her farmer-neighbors to be some of the most creative people I ever met. They built their own cabin from trees on their land, farmed herbs, vegetables, and fruit, built and maintained a pond stocked with fish. Carole's then husband re-purposed discarded farm implements, turning them into sculptures, mobiles and wind chimes. You might think that old silverware hanging on strings suspended from a rusted metal tractor wheel would never be pleasing to the ear and eye. Wrong. Deep Creatives like these tend not to walk around wearing labels like *artist* or *designer*.

In the wake of my New Warrior Training Adventure in October 1995, my life took a slight detour away from art into and the human potential movement that it has yet to return from. I admit I find it fascinating to discern what makes people grow and change, and what gets them stuck, unable to climb out of a rut.

Maybe I got stuck in my own rut with the judgment that "life is elsewhere." You know that one: everything I have is somehow insufficient or inadequate, including friends. Though it's been migrating slowly out of my consciousness over the last 25 years, remnants of that scarcity mindset still appear and, reliably, disappoint. That's part of the problem. Some of my friends, perhaps picking up on my own projections, my own disappointment, wonder why I would be friends with them. They know of my work and have inflated assumptions about the kind of success I am. Maybe we're a perfect match. In some unconscious way I may be looking down at them, while in an equally misplaced way they're looking up at me.

Over lunch recently, a friend of mine said, "I was always kind of surprised that you'd want to be friends with people like me and Paul. You know, average guys." I responded, "I've got to have friends! I always want to hang out with people I find warm, accepting, and funny." That's true. I have a deep need for the sharing and conviviality that ensues from social relations. But his question got me wondering. Did I substitute having friends of design for friends of expediency?

Cut to a friend's house when I was 20. We were smoking pot and listening to music. (This was 1975; can't that just go without saying?) It suddenly dawned on me, "Why am I here? I don't even like this guy!" Don't believe people when they tell you pot doesn't provide valuable epiphanies. My fellow drug dealer was a stunningly uninteresting guy. His job description was part of the problem. Drug dealers are not known for scintillating conversations and warm, heart-to-heart connections. Conversations are typically limited to "Man, this weed is good!" Cocaine was good for making you think you were having scintillating conversations. Alas, it meant more of the same: "Man, this coke is good!" Dealing drugs pretty much ensures that your conversations become delimited to dealing drugs, and your social group becomes delimited to drug dealers. Like breeds like, and drugs breed illusion.

I remember trying to convince my girlfriend that movies were more real than reality. Of course I was stoned. Even at the time I knew it was nonsense but, having never joined a debate club, I thought it would be an interesting argument to make, to see where it might lead. Aside from drug dealers, my best friends were film buffs who shared my obsessions. When we weren't watching films, we were discussing them, writing about them and reading about them.

I miss those days. I miss those conversations. I miss those people. Maybe it's just intellectual stimulation that I find lacking in friendships. It's rare today when I meet anyone well versed in film history with whom I can have an extended conversation about movies. I'm a terrible guy to go to the movies with since 90% of what's on offer doesn't interest me. I've never been a fan of the most popular Hollywood movies. My taste runs to the experimental and avant-garde, to norm-challenging forms and themes, hence my deeper appreciation for American independent and foreign cinema. I'm sure if I went online I could find innumerable chat groups to discuss cinema history and aesthetics but I long for those discussions as an element of friendship—the old-fashioned kind, person to person, face to face.

I also confess to an interest in celebrity circles. Established talent can be a great pool to discover a common well of creativity to augment creative juices. Smart people make smart people look smarter. They can also make less-smart people look, feel and become smarter. Living in NY or LA is convenient for making your way into circles like that. Even Moby, the accomplished composer and recording artist who lives in LA, commented on how he cultivates success partly so it will continue to win him invites to parties with other celebrities.

I've met a few along the way. Some are famous for being famous and display no discernible creative talents. But it's not the famous whose company I crave, not per se; it's celebrity Deep Creatives. Most are insanely talented. It is possible to create friendships with them. For reasons partly dating back to a computer crash in 2000 when I lost a lot of stars' home phone numbers, I've not succeeded in maintaining friendships with any. Post Hoop Dreams, I became friends with the incredibly talented actors Martha Plympton and Jennifer Jason-Leigh. I even offered Martha the lead role in my first feature. She appreciated how unusual the script was but turned it down because it required a nude scene. To my everlasting regret I never offered the part to Jennifer who would've been magnificent. Her name alone would've helped the film get distributed. Other stars I met along the way who I conceivably could have established friendships with include Gary Sinise, Tom Hanks, James Cameron, Faye Dunaway, Rip Torn, John Cusack, Randy Quaid, Wallace Shawn, Roger Ebert, Alec Baldwyn, Seymour Cassel, Spike Lee, and Joan Baez. For reasons unique to each, I blew it and came away with bupkis. At dinner with my girlfriend following the 1995 LA Spirit Awards, Julianne Moore came to our table and congratulated me on my win. Did I have the presence of mind to invite her to join us? Nope. Gary Sinise's wife was kind enough to invite us to their home in LA. I never followed up. I've put Richard Gere, Tim Meadows and Harry Lennix into three of my movies, but I couldn't get them on the phone now if my life depended on it. I also met the Dalai Lama, but I didn't think to ask for his number. Maybe the deeper truth is I didn't want connections with these Deep Creatives badly enough. Or maybe it was my old standby shadow: I'm not good enough.

That could be the bottom line. I want to be part of the in-crowd but I'm somehow deficient. My lifelong MO has made me the Outsider clamoring for a way in. You'd think I'd be good at knocking down doors. No. I tend to stand outside in the freezing rain until someone says, "Hey, stupid! Get out of the rain!" Yes, I have always related to Charlie Brown. I want to be recognized as a peer among Deep Creatives, have the door thrown wide, and be summarily welcomed in. You might think, well, didn't this happen with Hoop

Dreams? Of course the answer is yes. How many chances does one man get in a lifetime? Stay tuned, but that might have been it.

Before I go any further and lose the remaining friends I have, let me say that I love my friends. They're good people. I enjoy their company and, though I can't talk about film history or theory with them, we certainly talk philosophy and world affairs.

Maybe the truth is that other Deep Creatives, famous or not, are people just like me, too busy to spend time with brilliant friends discussing movies, philosophy, and the state of the world. They're busy creating art. They're not moaning about friendships.

Then there's my relationship with Harold Ramis which might belie this entire argument. Harold was a friend, mentor and colleague who even served for a number of years on my Warrior Films' board. Though I'm not sure he ever read my one comic screenplay—or maybe he was too kind to let on that he did read it and actually hated it—he honored me by sharing an unmade screenplay that he wrote based on his early life working in a hospital ward. In my own measured way, I told him that it wasn't very good. He agreed that it was not ready for prime time and likely never would be. That humility was one small part of all that he taught me and honored me with. I loved him and will celebrate him to my dying day.

Maybe Harold, in his own gentle way, now from beyond the grave, has returned to mentor me again and make me realize that this chapter is based on an entirely false premise. The notion that I never achieved my social network of Deep Creatives is nonsense. I've been too busy complaining about not having friends who are Deep Creatives to recognize I *did* have many, and still do. In rereading this chapter, I see now that this dawning realization contradicts the very premise I started with. Read closely and you'll see there's a seesawing, back and forth motion to the whole piece. "This didn't happen… Well, yes, actually, it did. I never achieved that… Hmm, truth be told, I guess I did." Let this chapter now stand as a textbook example of how a thesis can unravel as it's written; I have now thoroughly discredited the point I wanted to make. I hope I didn't fool you along the way!

So what does that leave me with? Gratitude. Immense gratitude. (OK, and some embarrassment.) Let me now publicly state I've had tremendously brilliant and talented friends my entire life. Regardless of where I've lived and when, I've always found people who are interesting and engaged, creating new forms, whether art or social inventions. I'm presently in two different writing groups, one founded by Maxine Hong Kingston who recently won the National Medal of Arts. She's been kind and generous to offer me advice and she blurbed one of my books. The renowned writer Pico Iyer said very kind things about my film *Journey from Zanskar* and we've exchanged email musings. Jack Kornfield wrote a deeply reflective and stirring Preface to my second book, and Ram Dass, not long before he died, said lovely things about my first book. Someday I'll write a fitting tribute to these and other brilliant Deep Creatives from my lifetime's accumulation, rather than back into it by starting off with a rant about them disappearing from my life or never appearing at all. Proof yet again that what goes through my head is not to be confused with any objective reality.

CHAPTER EIGHTEEN

My Life as a Lab Rat

I BECAME A LAB RAT AT AN EARLY AGE.

Though my own life has certainly been easier than most, it nonetheless started in misery. How to not let it end in misery is part of my strategic thinking. Like all children, I inherited the anxieties and confusions of my parents, mostly my mom's. After a miserable childhood, she spent a good deal of her lifetime suffering from worry. After she died, I read her journals from the two years in her 60s she spent in China as a teacher. In numerous entries, comprising an interminable catalog of slow-unfolding disaster with her boss, she wondered how getting fired could have come to pass. One simple question dropped out and hit me like a hammer. "Maybe I didn't worry enough?" I was dumbfounded. What?! Worry *enough*? What good does worry do? What good does *more* worry do that *some* worry alone can't accomplish? Which is to say, no matter what factor you multiply worry by it still ends up as zero. Maybe she should've considered burning her journals before she died because she clearly didn't worry enough about it falling into the wrong hands.

Her typical way of dealing with getting household repairs was to throw herself on the mercy of repairmen and contractors and beg for a low rate. Seeing the world from the perspective of anxiety and supplication didn't inspire confidence. Yet I inevitably inherited various predispositions to misery which took the same caste as her, that of Ashkenazi Jew. Neuroses, Weltschmertz and victimhood were the hallmarks of my upbringing. A German father? A Russian mother? I'm genetically predisposed to being paranoid and miserable. When I misplace my cell phone, I immediately think the worst. It was stolen and now a hacker in Kazakhstan is downloading my bank info.

My father died suddenly when I was nine, entombing all my yearning for his love and approval. The shock and depression pushed me to the starting line of a lifetime voyage: Happiness? Where is it? How to find it in the wake of life's challenges—death, disappointment, depression, heartbreak, illness, loss, betrayal, zits, athlete's foot and insolvency? Where to look to find fulfillment in life? Play sports all day, every day, and read Charlie Brown books? Those were the only solutions that spoke to me.

As I entered my teen years, I needed more. I looked at the options around me and they seemed empty and devoid of meaning. Working to make money to buy stuff seemed like the height of folly. When I was 17, I told my mother and siblings I wouldn't be buying Christmas presents for them anymore because I couldn't stand to buy things simply because societal conventions told me to. I was already the family black sheep, so they took it in stride. They still bought me gifts. I felt a bit guilty about that and told them they didn't need to. They're people with generous hearts—what are you going to do?

Other than food, drugs, sleep, travel, sex and music, I spent my teen years silently saying no to everything. Become a lawyer? A doctor? A scientist or engineer? A fireman or pilot? No thank you. Everywhere I looked I saw pathways through life that seemed unsuitable, mostly uninteresting, sometimes stultifying and empty. The high seas called to my sense of adventure, so I occasionally entertained the idea of becoming a merchant marine. Sailors got to see the world, leave a woman in every port, get bad tattoos and VD. The writing of Joseph Conrad and Malcolm Lowry beckoned. From them all I learned was that taking to the high seas might make you a great writer, but it won't necessarily make you happier. Joseph Conrad became one of the greatest writers ever but expressed plenty of doubts about whether true happiness was even possible. Malcolm Lowry died young as a miserable alcoholic.

I wondered if I shouldn't become a monk or a soldier. Maybe go live in a monastery for a while? Or let the Marines make a man out of me? Though I didn't opt for either, it was only years later that I understood the pull of each. I wanted to be initiated into mature masculinity. I wanted to be taught the discipline my father never had a chance to teach me, and military service was society's default mechanism for that. I also wanted a spiritual life, to be taught the reasons for living and dying.

I started reading books my parents left lying around the house. Edward Albee's play *The Zoo Story* fascinated me, but it seemed to be pointing in the opposite direction from happiness. The *Bhagavad Gita* carried significant clues, but I didn't have the sophistication to recognize what they were. Alan Watts' *The Book* was my first experience of a light bulb turning on. The everyday world is constructed out of dualities. Of course! But those dualities are momentary appearances, not ever-present, underlying realities. OK... It was clear and concise and made a lot of sense. But how does one access the non-dual? How does one incorporate these ideas so they become a feature of everyday life? The book didn't say, and I didn't know where to find out.

I defaulted to studying myself. "I'll become my own lab rat. I'll analyze my own life to see if I can learn what it is that creates lasting happiness. What actions are required? How to distinguish them from those that bring pain and suffering?" I didn't know what else to do. I had no adults to guide me, no mentors. My mom was busy worrying, consumed by her many challenges and dramas. Where to turn? Finding lasting happiness is not part of everyday conversation. It doesn't show up in headlines or on the evening news. Friends don't typically chat about it while devouring after-school snacks. I couldn't even articulate the questions I wanted to ask. I had no choice but to try to figure it out on my own, to use my own life to see what worked and what didn't. My experiment in living took shape.

Was I conscious of this strategy? Not remotely. But I was nonetheless fully committed. So much suffering in the world, mine and others'. There must be something that can be done. Given how suddenly and randomly I knew that death could come, I was highly motivated. I got pulled in the direction of every interesting new thought or question that crossed my path. Finding clues in scraps, I tried to hack out a single trail through the deepening jungle of ideas and experiences, to construct a set of working behaviors.

"Scientists say you can wipe off 80% of the water on your body before using your towel." I can't remember where I read that, but it made sense to me. "If you blot your skin with a towel rather than rub it your skin will always stay creamy and soft." My high school girlfriend told me that one. I still practice both. Not everything I picked up had to do with toweling off after showers.

Along with useful guideposts, I picked up a lot of ridiculous notions because I thought at the time they might prove meaningful for the persona I was developing. At 15, I resolved to stop wearing underwear. What caught my attention was some rock star talking about how sex with strangers was made easier. I was certainly looking forward to having sex, so I thought I better get prepared. I don't know if I even liked the guy's music. These random clues felt like runes delivered from the universe. For years, I played basketball, swam, biked and jogged without a jockstrap or underwear. I thought it was cool. It's a wonder my genitals remained functional. This habit persisted until my 23rd year when, after repeated bouts of doubling over in agony for half a day, I finally connected the wrenching pain in my balls to the lack of support they were receiving. You'd think regularly herniated testicles might create their own unforgettable lessons but I'm a slow learner.

I absorbed whatever influences I happened across. I still remember how one morning 45 years ago my friend Ben decided to make himself a second plate of fried eggs because the first tasted so good. I was stunned. You can make yourself seconds?! Maybe I was just amazed at his easeful exuberance, or maybe that was my introduction to the concept of abundance. The lesson could encompass a sports idol commenting offhand how he preferred tea to coffee. A politician might remark that his favorite place to vacation in the Caribbean was Jamaica because the music was best. A successful entrepreneur might explain that if he didn't get up every day at 5:00 he'd never accomplish half his daily tasks. (That one is used purely for illustrative purposes. I never get up every day at 5.)

Another strange notion I adopted was sleeping without a pillow. I probably saw it in a Western somewhere. Some scene out on the open range where the tough and brawny hero admonishes a young cowboy for fluffing clothes under his head on the cold and barren ground. In my head, I can hear John Wayne saying "Only girls need pillows" to Montgomery Clift, though I don't think *Red River* has any such scene. This is the kind of bogus instruction that can arise when you let your life be guided by movie icons.

I hit college thinking if I learned as much as I could from the world's great thinkers and philosophers surely that knowledge would lead to happiness. Life, I quickly discovered, is "solitary, poor, nasty, brutish, and short." Thank you, Thomas Hobbes! Reading him in my first semester political philosophy class probably contributed to my later pivot to film studies.

Turns out I did learn something important from reading the great thinkers and philosophers. I learned that I don't have the intellectual capacity to understand the world's great thinkers and philosophers. Much later, I also learned that I should have turned from the Renaissance philosophers to the ancient Greeks, particularly Aristotle, Socrates, and the stoics, who wrote a lot about happiness. They used the term Eudaimonia which really doesn't translate as happiness; it denotes a life well-lived, while the Greek term *philosophia* means love of wisdom. Both terms suit me. Though I continued to utilize the word happiness, in a sense I did become a philosopher as I went forward. I became the philosopher of my own life. If this book doesn't convince you, I don't know what will.

Stuck on a college pre-law track, I was enacting the conventional wisdom that it is what you do that opens the pathway to happiness. What career you pursue can be an important element, but it's not the end-all, be-all. Unlike the Greeks, I was also focused on fun. Films provided it. After two years I gave up on the notion of law school and focused almost exclusively on film history and criticism. A pathway opened. I could be a film critic! Make a living telling people what I thought about movies? Are you kidding me? My fellow University of Illinois alum Roger Ebert did it following an almost identical path. It felt like the Yellow Brick Road.

I was unconsciously doing something I only learned a name for years later. "Follow your bliss," Joseph Campbell taught. The bliss I got from watching and writing about movies, later transitioning into making them, was enormous. Though it took many more years, I finally came to identify myself as an artist. That was a relief. At last, I had a proper noun to use as a label, and a social role I could use to explain myself to others. I loved making movies; I loved sharing them with others. It created great happiness. That was gratifying. But it was still not *it*. Getting my films financed, made and distributed created heaps of misery in its own right. I couldn't understand it. If I was doing what I was certain was my life's calling, why was I still miserable?

Maybe I was gay and didn't realize it? That question took about 10 years to resolve. Following work with my therapist it eventually became clear that it was my feelings that needed to come out of the closet, not my sexual orientation.

Does having as many interesting life experiences as possible make for happiness? Somehow by the age of 22 I intuited "No," maybe as a result of my misadventures detailed in *At Sea*. Out of some deep interior place of knowing, these lyrics spilled out of me:

> *"I'm an experiential groupie, a consumer of events.*
> *I like my breakfast with a Happening.*
> *Break for an afternoon of sense.*
> *My evening's spent preparing for the night's experience!"*

Life experiences per se, no matter how exciting and dramatic, are ephemeral, empty of lasting value. But it took a lot of convincing. I traveled widely, even into my 40s—to India, Iran, China, Egypt, Korea, Thailand, Morocco and everywhere in Europe. All those trips satisfied my wanderlust and eventually helped me understand myself as a drama queen, but didn't add up to happiness. The ultimate emptiness of experience was reinforced years later when I went to the Oscars and Emmys and received supreme career validations. As honored as I was to be nominated for those prestigious awards, the affairs themselves proved less than joyful, more suited for an anthropology class—20th Century Celebrity Culture: How the fame economy became a fixture of late capitalism.

Eventually, my beliefs in the way things are, and should be, also had to go. Beliefs themselves are the problem. They are a source of misery. Name any belief you hold dear, any ideology, and at some point, often quickly, most reveal themselves to be partial, conditional truths. Remember, the world was known to be absolutely flat. Later, Newtonian physics was the gold standard. One hundred years ago, it was impossible to conceive of the Earth heating up. Be careful what you place your faith and judgment in; time makes fools of us all. "The meek shall inherit the earth." Doubtful. "The arc of the moral universe is long, but it bends toward justice." I could only wish. "Everyone deserves a fair shake." True enough, but it has yet to happen in the last 10,000 years of human history and likely won't soon.

My family raised me to believe all answers could be found in rationality and critical thinking. Nope. As with science and belief, so with logic. Thinking my way to solutions was inadequate. In fact, my thinking mind could be part of the problem, the main part. I awoke to the understanding that no matter how bright I was, intelligence alone could never usher a person into a lifetime of happiness (and given an early and mighty launch into hubris, it took me a while to realize I wasn't all that bright). I should've known that from living with my mom who was pretty smart, but I was clueless at the time to draw that conclusion. Now much of what makes me happy is recognizing that much of what goes through my mind, especially judgments, is of little to no value. Most of the time so-called good sense is nonsense.

First men's work, and later dharma, taught me that emotions—all that is going on in the feeling body—are an essential component to happiness and must be incorporated into solutions. They are pillars of 360-degree awareness. This became revelatory. Trying to resolve trauma without incorporating emotions is a waste of time. But as revelatory as uncovering my emotions was, that too was an answer not everlasting. People become bound by their emotions, straitjacketed, thinking those feelings are fundamental to who they are, inseparable from their core. How many times do you need to expunge the anger and grief about what Dad did to you as a kid before moving on? Yes, those wounds reappear, even regularly, but that doesn't mean that the emotions attached to them are always going to surface, that there's something unshakable and eternal about them. It becomes a question of identification. If we identify with them, if they're part of the story we tell ourselves about who we are, then yes, they'll come and go and come again. But that story can and does change. Can we be open to a new one? What about no story at all? New informed choices that are well-placed and well-timed can reroute and even evaporate emotions. Despite what VA doctors sometimes tell their Veteran patients, PTS is not everlasting.

As with emotions, so with personality and character. No lasting or eternal value there. "You" are not you. Just as the history of our wounds no longer exists in the present, self-identity is a mental construct. Though it's important to develop a healthy ego in your teens, it can become as much a detriment to happiness as a support in later life. Foiled again!

Finally, at 32, I stumbled into the practice of dharma and it changed everything. Known as The Middle Way for very good reasons, it refutes the pathway of abstinence at one extreme and equally refutes the pathway of hedonic pleasure at the other. Steer to the middle. Everything in moderation—including, occasionally, moderation. Once I got on that path there was no turning back. The answers I sought were there. The Buddha wasn't referred to as a physician at times for no reason.

Buddhism helps me focus on what the real building blocks for happiness are—starting with accepting fundamental realities. Seeing how reality unfolds does not require belief in reality. Or Buddhism. Or anything else. You just see what happens and accept it. "Oh, so that's reality right now." I accept these new realities, ever-evolving, ceaselessly changing, rather than fearing the eradication of things I cling to. I accept the co-dependent origination of all things rather than ceaselessly spinning in an orbit of my own creation, assuming my hurts and worries are somehow unique. I accept suffering as an entirely normal part of life rather than assuming adversity precludes the possibility of happiness. I accept that ideas and concepts and beliefs are not lasting verities, much less anything to try to hold dearly to.

Helpfully, the Buddha laid out a very practical road map for us: the Eightfold Path. Right livelihood, right view, right intention, right mindfulness, right speech, right action, right effort and finally, right concentration (stabilizing the mind regardless of vicissitudes). To explore each of these aspects fully is beyond my scope here. Suffice it to say that the Eightfold Path is the Buddha's highway to happiness.

Every morning I recite these words as part of my Zen service:

> *I rely upon selfless awareness. I do not rely upon concepts of self and other that appear. I do not depend upon beliefs, sensations, and emotions which arise and fall away. Meditative awareness, clear intention, acting wisely, compassionately and skillfully are this practice. I rely upon this only. I rely upon this ceaselessly.*

These statements *are* everlasting and true. These are realities you can build a lifetime of happiness on.

I'm learning now to be *in* the world but not *of* it, how to experience wonderful things but not need them, how to have a strong identity but not identify with it, how to suffer but not wallow in suffering, how to think critically but not assume those judgments to be true, how to love and know love is not forever, how to happily invest time, energy, and money in people, ventures, and projects, and know they'll all dissolve, disappear, or die. I'm learning how to be happy when the sun is shining or there is rain, when I feel strong and fit or have the flu, when my diabetes is under control or when it's not, when the Golden State Warriors win or lose, when my landlord won't fix my broken tub or raises my rent, when I sign a film streaming deal or Netflix blows me off, when Hoop Dreams earns another round of royalties or my partners deny me public recognition again, when someone's leaning on their car horn for over a minute (as I write this) or when there's blessed silence, even when I lose my late wife to cancer.

Rather than put my faith in things that do not last, I do my best to rest in the reality of ceaseless change and the fact that there is nothing remotely everlasting or eternal about Frederick Marx—what my ego tells me is *me*. As Trungpa Rinpoche pointed out, we are perpetually falling with nothing to hold on to. But the good news is there is no ground. Happiness waits for us in flight. I guess there's nothing left to do now but go and get enlightened.

So I'm trying, even when I recognize that *waking up* occurs just as equally through not trying. My girlfriend has a tendency to ask me questions about choices that carry no import for me. "Should we have dinner at 5 or 6? Should we go to Pascale's or Tres Hombres? Should we invite friends to our place or go to theirs?" It's rare that I have a preference. More often than not I'll say, "I'm happy either way."

One day I took special note of that. Though I was in no way consciously extending my dharma practice, I recognized my response as good practice indeed. So I took to underscoring it when she would ask me questions. "You know me, I'm happy all the time, no matter what!" The act of saying it constitutes a lovely practice in its own right. It's also a lovely joke. I'm *not* happy all the time of course. We both know that, so it's funny. It's become a tagline that reliably makes us laugh.

But I'm working on making it true. If I already recognize that through much of the day "I'm happy either way," why not extrapolate that to 24/7? Now when I say "I'm happy no matter what," the joke still elicits a smile from us both while simultaneously asserting a conviction about myself I'm in the process of making true. Maybe similar to "Fake it 'til you make it." It's delighting me and becoming truer with each iteration.

My own preferences for *this* over *that* are fading. I like to play a game with the food I have on hand in the house—pretending that it's all I have for the coming days to survive. Finishing every last morsel before going shopping is one of the rules. Peanut butter and jelly? Fine. Week-old chicken? Just slather on the mayonnaise. Old lettuce? Blue cheese dressing makes everything tasty. I don't make a fetish out of eating the latest, hottest, coolest new dishes from the latest, hottest, coolest chefs and restaurants. Welcoming and accepting all that arises expands and opens me, loosening the hold that personality has on my life. I relish whatever's available.

I'm only 69 and hopefully have a long way to go, but preliminary results from my experiment indicate success. Maybe it's a safe bet now that my life will not end in misery. Of course, you never know what kick in the balls might be lurking around the next corner, what new experiments life will serve up next to get this rat wandering once more through the maze. Remember lab rats don't always make it through. The only certainty is uncertainty! Crazy and true, but now strangely reassuring.

CHAPTER NINETEEN

Against Hope

Wish in one hand and shit in the other and see which one fills up first.

—Anonymous

"You're against hope? What?! Are you a complete cynic? A bomb throwing nihilist?! A Devil worshiper? How can you be against hope?!!"

This is the reaction I sometimes get when I have the courage to share my thoughts on this issue. My friend Chris first turned me on to this idea. Giving credit where credit is due, I'd tell you his full name but I don't want the hate mail directed at him.

Taking a stand against hope might be a very Zen position to take. Which is ironic, given that Zen is really about not taking positions on anything.

Why am I against hope? I'm now 69 years old and over the course of my lifetime I've seen relationships people have with each other and with the natural world degrade enormously. I grew up in the 60s and 70s when it seemed anything was possible. Now when I look at the status quo of wealth inequality worldwide, increasing threats of nuclear and climate holocausts, the twilight of democracy and the accelerating control autocrats have over people and the world's resources, hope is an illusion I can no longer indulge in.

Hope is the ideological handmaiden of colonialism. It was hope that was sold to African slaves and Native Americans in the form of Christianity. They were told life is hard because they were born into sin. But hold on! They could still hope to go to heaven where they'd live in paradise. Different religions sell this same bill of goods to people worldwide—to people suffering and toiling in misery.

So people learn to cling to hope as if to a lifesaver. But it's a lifesaver full of holes: hope based on religious belief or outright fantasy. "The Second Coming is upon us." "The UN will figure something out." "Space aliens will save us." Personally, I don't think the combined efforts of Santa Claus, the Tooth Fairy, and Glenda, the Good Witch of the North will be sufficient to halt what is now clearly irreversible climate change.

Why invest time wishing for an alternate reality? Whatever you hope for, even if it comes to pass, will change again. Isn't it better to be equanimous with what's here now? Some say we have to be able to envision a new world in order to bring it into creation. Yes. But doesn't intention fulfill that objective? Let's build our plans and work toward that new world with *practicalities*. Rather than teaching people to hope for a better afterlife, how 'bout we work hard to improve their present living conditions?

Maybe it comes down to semantics—how you define hope; how you define intention. Possibly. Vaclav Havel said, "Hope is not the conviction that something will turn out well. It is the certainty that something is worth doing no matter how it turns out." To me, that's just confusing hope with intention. But I'm not going to split those hairs. I'll just point out that hope may well be the greatest drug being sold on the world market today. Political parties couldn't survive without selling hope. Corporations, not just greeting card companies, make millions selling hope. "Buying an electric car is hope for the future." "Install hope on your roof with solar panels." If hope were exposed as the illusion it is, pure future projection, is it possible that, following the initial jolt of despair, people might experience renewed intentionality about making needed changes in the world? Embracing realism, facing reality, should not be a prescription for euthanasia. It's the logical place to begin, the *only* place from which we can truly start to make functional change.

Sometimes I wish people would lose all hope, because many hopes seem to be based in a misplaced trust in people and behaviors that are proven destructive. A lot of people used to put their faith in Elon Musk until he came out of the closet as a fascist, intent on dismantling democracy and civic culture. Maybe now we can support him in moving to Mars. A common expression I've heard for years is "Technology will save us." Oh yeah? Isn't technology a big part of what got us into this mess? As Wes Jackson teaches us, technological fundamentalism is an existential threat even greater than religious fundamentalism. It is a belief system now two hundred years old, no less deep-seated in the culture of the West than thousand-year-old religions in cultures of the East. Jackson thinks it's going to take a whole new paradigm of thinking and behavior to get us out of it, some of which is neatly summarized in his simple term down-powering. As Einstein supposedly but didn't actually say: "We cannot solve problems from the same level of thinking that created them." Regardless of where the statement came from, I think it's true.

Hope is food intake without value. There's no sustenance, no nourishment. Like hard candy, it has all the lasting worth of a sugar high. Just like with drugs. You may get a delicious momentary rush but eventually you'll come down and find yourself in the same old place, maybe even worse off than you were before. Most people are hope addicts. It's time to go cold turkey.

I have no hope that politics in this country will ever *not* be about self-interest. I have no hope that the world's 3,300 billionaires, holding 12-trillion dollars in assets, will one day wake up and give away most of their money to the billions of people around the world who could do really productive and useful things with it. I have no hope that the worldwide economy will suddenly shift from carbon extraction toward sustainable energy and soil and water conservation. I have no hope that military contractors will suddenly decide "Our business is evil. We have to stop being merchants of death and produce things that are healthy and wholesome for people." I have no hope that one day this country will provide low-cost cradle to grave health care for every American. I have no hope that working people everywhere will suddenly be given a living wage and treated with safe working conditions, dignity and respect. I have no hope that children everywhere will be offered free quality education. I have no hope that people will suddenly awaken from the dream of "me, myself, and I," grabbing for all the spoils they can, and recognize our very survival depends on each other. None of this will happen, not in my lifetime. I've given up hope.

Most people assume when you make statements like that you've given up, period. Wrong. It helps me discern all that needs to be done. Giving up hope helps me clarify intentions. Hoping is passive; setting intentions is active. I'm not sitting back and hoping things will change, but setting clear and achievable intentions to ensure they come to pass. Intentions demand action. It's about going to work to bring needed changes to fruition.

Despair is the shadow companion of hope. Just take a close look over time at someone who is hopeful, and you will often see a person regularly feeling despair. Personally, I want to get off the see-saw, to stop swinging between extremes. Sure, you can feel both when looking at the world today. And yes, to some degree it depends on where you look. But what if we get off that roller coaster altogether? No more going up with hope and down with despair. What if we gaze upon all that exists with the same accepting, compassionate gaze? What if we learn to read inspiring examples of positive change by the world's every Dalai Lama or Bishop Tutu, and at the same time stay open to horrifying examples of ignorance and destruction from the latest reports of war in Ukraine and bombings in Gaza and say yes to them all? "Yes. Such is life."

Acceptance does not mean approval. It does not mean complacency. It does not mean giving in to a lifestyle of apathy and disillusionment. It just means clear acknowledgment of the common ground we all inhabit. We have to start from a recognition of *what is* before we can co-create *what should be*.

To heal the world's divisions we need whole new ways of thinking and behaving, and I think embracing reality can jump-start us into that new paradigm. I place my trust in reality, however complex, contradictory, and confounding, likewise surprising and magical. The endless mysterious unfolding of what's true, what's actually happening, demands my constant attention. So I jettison beliefs. If we could encourage people to inquire more deeply into what's happening at any given time and place, they might give up their own belief systems altogether.

There's a wonderful saying: "Forgiveness is letting go of all hope for a better past." How true. For me, equanimity is letting go of all hope for a better future. Working together from that place of tranquility, facing and accepting some very hard realities and setting very clear intentions, we can move forward and make this a better world for everyone.

How about we aim to make heaven here on Earth? If we equitably distribute available resources like food, clothing, shelter, health care and education, we'll establish a solid ground of universal opportunity for human beings to begin building their own meaningful futures. We know everything will change. So, let's start out and see what happens. And keep building until we understand how any initial plans might need to be adapted. I rest my energy, thinking and planning on change. In hope you can never rest. However paradoxical it may sound, it *is* possible to rest in ceaseless change. That's where you'll find me... hopefully!

Epilogue

One should [...] be able to see that things are hopeless and yet be determined to make them otherwise.

—F. Scott Fitzgerald

Thank You for Reading My Book

I hope you've appreciated *Confessions of a Sacred Fool*—my second collage of mini-essays. I dramatically failed at putting everything I had to say into that first volume. There could be more. God help us all.

Before you go and start confessing your own sacred foolishness, I have a small favor to ask: Could you please write an Amazon review? Even if it's only one or two sentences, your review means a lot.

Reviews are the best way for "small" books like this one to get noticed and reach a wider audience. For this reason, your support really does make a difference.

Simply go to this book's Amazon page, scroll down, and click "Write a customer review." Even if you did not buy the book from Amazon, you might still be able to sneak a review past their diabolical algorithmic censors.

If you prefer audiobooks, stay tuned. I should have this book and my previous one available shortly. Consider it my audition for a future in stand-up comedy.

Thanks again for reading. I wish you much fulfillment in your journey, especially now that you can drop a few Absurdities and Wisdoms on your friends and family!

Smiling,

Frederick Marx

Acknowledgments

Two writers' groups have been indispensable in helping me understand and accept myself as an author. First is the Bay Area Veterans Writers Group, founded by Maxine Hong Kingston in 1993, which I joined in 2016. Though I don't measure up to the quality of highbrow work these writers produce, many of them professionals, I take comfort in our esprit de corps, rituals of conscious practice, and the abundance of encouraging feedback.

Bob Golling, a Veteran (in both senses of the word) of that founding group, also started the Placer County Writers. We meet weekly at the Flower Farm Cafe in Loomis, CA, where, regardless of the weather, regardless of sitting inside or outside, it's always sunny and warm. I'm grateful for the ever-changing, ever-deepening community that results from the regular sharing of our work. I'm also grateful for the many practical suggestions and hearty laughter that greeted this book's early draft chapters.

Ryan Cove gave me encouraging comments and valuable suggestions during his creative edit review. He graciously paid for the excellent copyediting services of Robyn Rae Brundage, whose scrupulousness forced me to re-examine every word, phrase, and punctuation mark, and she then hung in there with me as I scrupulously over-thought it all.

My partner Maggie Perkins has once again proven indispensable to my publishing process. She got me to experiment with AI for new book titles and cover designs. If you're grateful that the title of this sequel to my last book does not contain the word *turds* you can thank her.

Other Works by Frederick Marx

BOOKS

Turds of Wisdom (2023)
Rites to a Good Life (2020)
At Death Do Us Part (2018)

FILMS

It's Your Wonderful Life! (in progress)
Veterans Journey Home: a five-part series (2023)
- *Kalani's Story*
- *Leaving it on the Land*
- *Solutions*
- *On Black Mountain*
- *Ben's Story*

Rites of Passage (2018)
The Tatanka Alliance (2015)
Journey from Zanskar (2010)
Boys to Men: a four-part series (2004)
- *Are You Listening?*
- *Spencer's Story*
- *Al-Tran's Story*
- *Cisco's Story*

The Unspoken (1999)
Saving the Sphinx (Producer only, 1997)
Joey Skaggs: Bullshit & Balls (1996)
A Hoop Dreams Reunion (1995)
Hoop Dreams (1994)
Higher Goals (1993)
Inside/Out (1991)
Out of the Silence (Co-Producer, Editor only, 1991)
Hiding Out for Heaven (1990)
Dreams from China (1989)
House of UnAmerican Activities (1984)
Dream Documentary (1981)

www.ingramcontent.com/pod-product-compliance
Lightning Source LLC
Chambersburg PA
CBHW030219170426
43194CB00007BA/795